STORIES
WE BROUGHT
WITH US

SECOND EDITION

STORIES WE BROUGHT WITH US

Beginning Readings

CAROL KASSER
ANN SILVERMAN

Prentice Hall Regents
Englewood Cliffs, New Jersey 07632

Stories we brought with us: beginning readings / [compiled by] Carol Kasser, Ann Silverman. — 2nd ed.
p. cm.
Rev. and updated ed. of: Stories we brought with us / Carol Kasser, Ann Silverman.
ISBN 0-13-122-145-0
1. English language—Textbooks for foreign speakers. 2. Readers. 3. Tales. I. Kasser, Carol. II. Silverman, Ann. III. Kasser, Carol Stories we brought with us.
PE1128.K35 1994
428.6'4—dc20

94-7318
CIP

Acquisitions editor: *Nancy Baxer*
Editorial production/design manager: *Dominick Mosco*
Editorial/production supervision
 and interior design: *Christine McLaughlin Mann*
Production Coordinator: *Ray Keating*

Cover Design Coordinator: *Merle Krumper*
Cover Design: *Marianne Frasco*
Electronic Art: *Todd Ware, Rolando Corujo*

Interior Art: Ona Kalstein

©1994 by Prentice Hall Regents
Prentice-Hall, Inc.
A Simon & Schuster Company
Englewood Cliffs, New Jersey 07632

Printed in the United States of America

10   9   8   7   6   5   4

ISBN   0-13-122145-0

Printed on Recycled Paper

Prentice-Hall International (UK) Limited, *London*
Prentice-Hall of Australia Pty. Limited, *Sydney*
Prentice-Hall Canada Inc., *Toronto*
Prentice-Hall Hispanoamericana, S.A., *Mexico*
Prentice-Hall of India Private Limited, *New Delhi*
Prentice-Hall of Japan, Inc., *Tokyo*
Simon & Schuster Asia Pte. Ltd., *Singapore*
Editora Prentice-Hall do Brasil, Ltda., *Rio de Janeiro*

CONTENTS

n

a

TO THE TEACHER

The idea for this book came from our students' interest in reading and telling stories that were handed down to them by their parents, grandparents, and teachers in their own countries. Some of the stories in this collection may already be familiar to your students; others may not be. We hope that students will react to the stories, ask questions, make comments, tell other versions, and finally relate stories from their own countries.

Each story in this book has two versions. Version A uses less complex structures and more limited vocabulary. Version B uses a greater variety of structures and is more idiomatic. Telling the story twice allows the students to grasp the story line and characters in version A so that when they read version B, they can be more attentive to structure and vocabulary. Accordingly, each story also has two sets of exercises. We don't recommend that all students do all of the exercises; you will want to decide which exercises are appropriate for your students. For example, all students can do "Before You Start to Read," which is found before the *A* version of each story, and "Topics for Discussion/ Writing," which is usually at the end of the *B* version.

Questions marked (*) require students to compare one story to another story in the book. There are many exercises, too, that require higher-level cognitive skills, such as making inferences, drawing conclusions, comparing stories, and making analogies, because we recognize that many students with low reading levels in English have high-level thinking skills that are rarely challenged by most low-level ESL readers.

In addition to the exercises we have included, you may want to try the following activities with your classes.

1. Dictation After students have read and are familiar with the story, dictate a paragraph one sentence at a time, at normal speed. As an alternative, do a cloze dictation using a mimeographed paragraph with every nth word deleted.

2. Read and Look Up To encourage students to read at the sentence level rather than word by word, ask them to read a sentence or short paragraph and then look up. Then ask for information from that sentence or paragraph.

3. Rewrite Ask the students to rewrite the story, either individually or in groups.

4. Retell Ask students to retell the story, either orally or in writing. They may want to use the illustrations in the book as a guide. (You will notice that the illustrations for "The Ant and the Cicada," page 27, form a sequence that tells the complete story.) Try retelling this story first if students have difficulty remembering details and sequence.

Learning to read in a second language is often hard work. But we think that it can be a source of pleasure and satisfaction—even for beginning students. Sharing stories and folktales is one way to encourage such enjoyment.

ACKNOWLEDGMENTS

We wish to express our gratitude to the following people: Virginia French Allen and Francis Shoemaker, Spring Institute, CO; Marilyn Funk, Jones Middle School, Philadelphia, PA; Matilde Garcia, Inter-American University, Puerto Rico; Lucy Ogburn, Middlesex Community College, MA; Patt Rigg, Reading Consultant, Tucson, AZ; Leigh Tischler, Montgomery County, MD Public Schools; Ramona Trujillo, Toledo, OH Public Schools; Suzanne Vernon, Community College of Philadelphia, PA; Greta Vollmer, High School of International Studies, San Francisco, CA; and last, but not least, our students, who brought these stories with them.

Carol Kasser
Ann Silverman

A Lesson in Persistence

Before you start to read

○ Look at the picture. Do you think the story will be about a young person or about an old person? A man or a woman? Modern times or old times? Explain why you think so.

○ The title says this story will teach you a lesson. As you read the story, try to guess what the lesson is.

○ *Persistence* means continuing to do something for a long time, even when other people think you are wrong or foolish. Can you think of something you persist in doing because you know it is right? Can you think of something you or others persist in doing even though it is wrong?

○ Is persistence always good? What do you think about each of the following?

  a. an athlete who persists in practicing

  b. a child who persistently asks for candy

  c. a persistent cough

  d. a dog that barks persistently

  e. someone who tries persistently to find a job

○ As you read, decide whether the old man's persistence is good or bad. Be prepared to explain your answer.

1

A Lesson in Persistence

A Lesson in Persistence

1   A long time ago, there was an old man who was very patient. Every day, he sat in front of his house doing the same job. He was patiently sharpening a piece of iron.

2   One day his neighbor saw him at work. He asked the man, "What are you doing?" The old man said, "I want to make this iron into a needle."

3   The neighbor was surprised because the piece of iron was big, and a needle is very small. He asked the man "How long will it take you to finish making the needle?'

4   The old man answered, "I don't know. If I die before I finish, I will leave this work for my son. And if my son dies before it is finished, he will leave this work for my grandchildren. Someday, this piece of iron will be a needle."

Exercises

Word Choice

Choose from the following prepositions to fill in the blanks.

at	**for**	**in**
into	**of**	**from**

1. The old man was _____ work.

2. He had a piece _____ iron.

3. He wanted to make it _____ a needle.

4. He might have to leave this work _____ his son.

5. This story gives us a lesson _____ persistence.

Use the related forms of each word to fill in the blanks.

patience   **patient**   **patiently**

1. It is important to have _____ with children.

2. You must be very _____ when you study a new language.

3. Joe worked slowly and _____ on the assignment.

persist   **persistent**   **persistently**   **persistence**

1. If you study _____, you will learn English.

2. Sometimes it is hard to _____ in your studies when you have other things to do.

3. But with a little _____ you can learn
   English and do well in school.

4. If you are _____, all of your hard work will
   pay off.

surprise   **surprised**   **surprising**   **surprisingly**

1. The cat _____ me when it jumped on me.

2. There is a _____ for you on the desk.

3. Betty and Jill did _____ well in the race.

4. It is _____ how well you can do if you persist.

Reading from Context

Look at the original sentences in the story to guess the meaning of
the underlined words in the following sentences.
   1. "The old man responded, 'I don't know.'"(paragraph 4)
   2. "Daily, he sat in front of his house doing the same task."
      (paragraph 1)
   3. "If my son dies before it is completed, he will leave this work
      for my grandchildren." (paragraph 4)

Idiom Practice

Notice this idiom with *take*: "How long will it take you to finish?"
Practice that idiom by asking your classmates these questions and
reporting their answers to the class.
   ○ How long does it take you to go home from school every day?
   ○ How long did it take you to eat your dinner last night?
   ○ How long does it take you to get dressed in the morning?
   ○ How long will it take you to complete your courses?
   ○ How long would it take you to save enough money for a car?

Punctuation

Copy these sentences, adding punctuation and changing small letters to capital letters as needed.

1. what are you doing the old mans neighbor asked

   _____

2. the old man said if i die before the work is finished my son will finish it

   _____

Sounds and Spellings

Ten of the following words contain the /sh/ sound. Can you find these ten? (*Hint:* Say each word, and listen for the /sh/ sound somewhere in the word.)

finished	grandchildren	lesson	machine	national
ocean	patiently	surely	racial	sharpening
special	permission	teacher	which	surprised

Homophones are same-sound words with different spellings, like *here* and *hear*. English has hundreds of homophones, including

I, eye	no, know	piece, peace
so, sew	too, two	would, wood

Find the correct word from that list to fill in each blank. Write or print that word in the blank.

> **Example:** The doctor told me to close my right ____eye____.

1. A bicycle has _____ wheels.

2. Where _____ you like to go?

3. People use needles when they _____.

4. The old man had a _____ of iron.

5. We don't _____ the man's name.

6. We get _____ from trees.

7. Tell me yes or _____.

8. Patricia was tired, _____ she sat down.

9. Candy is sweet, and cake is, _____.

10. Why is there war when everyone wants _____?

A Lesson in Persistence

1   Long ago there lived an old man who sat patiently working in his front yard every day. He was slowly sharpening a piece of iron. His only tool was a file.

2   One day his neighbor saw him at work and asked him what he was doing. The old man explained that he wanted to make the iron into a needle.

3   The neighbor was very surprised to hear that because the the piece of iron was very big, and a needle is very, very tiny. He asked, "Won't it take many years to finish making the needle?"

4   The old man responded that he did not know how long it would take to finish the job of making the needle. But if he died before it was completed, he would leave the work for his son. And if his son died before it was finished, he would leave it for his grandchildren. Someday the piece of iron would become a needle.

Exercises

Sentence Meanings

Which sentences say something that is *True* according to the story?
Which sentences say something *False*?

True–False

1. _____ The old man's only tool was a needle.
2. _____ The old man worked quickly.
3. _____ The old man was patient.
4. _____ The old man might not finish the job himself.
5. _____ The old man was persistent.

Word Meanings

Match the words in the first column with their definitions in the
second column.

1. _____ completed   a. a tool used to grind or smooth
2. _____ explained   b. asked
3. _____ file   c. an instrument used to do a
                              special job
4. _____ responded   d. answered
5. _____ sharpening   e. making a point or edge
6. _____ tiny   f. gave reasons for; made clear
7. _____ tool   g. the area around a house or
                              building
8. _____ yard   h. finished
                          i. needle
                          j. very small
                          k. surprised

Three words in each of the following groups have almost the same meaning. Circle the word that has a very different meaning. You may use a dictionary, if necessary.

1. make   produce   take   create

2. answer   finish   reply   respond

3. surprised   amazed   afraid   astonished

4. old   happy   ancient   elderly

5. working   laboring   toiling   asking

Circle the words that are similar.

1. Which of the following are tools?

files   **hammers**   **yards**
neighbors   **tables**   **saws**

2. Which of the following are metals?

copper   **cotton**   **gold**   **meat**
iron   **silver**   **tin**   **wood**

3. Which of the following are people?

babies   **cars**   **daughters**   **grandchildren**
needles   **sons**   **neighbors**

Words in Context

Choose from the following words to fill in the blanks:

finished   **helping**   **iron**   **surprised**
likely   **needle**   **neighbor**

neighborhood	patiently	persistence
piece	harp	sharpening

1. The man worked _____ at his job.

2. Jim was _____ his knife so that it would cut better.

3. Amy was using a _____ to sew a dress.

4. It is important to have _____ when you do a difficult job.

5. My _____ lives across the street.

6. Virginia was very _____ when she saw her present.

7. Have you _____ your homework yet?

8. Would you like a _____ of candy?

9. We use _____ in making steel.

10. Is there a library in your _____?

Use the context of a sentence to guess the meaning of a word.

1. Look at paragraph 3 to guess the meaning of the underlined words in the following passage.

   The neighbor was very <u>amazed</u> to hear that, because the piece of iron was huge and a needle is small.

2. Look at paragraph 4 to find the meaning of the underlined words in the following passage.

   The old man <u>replied</u> that he <u>was unsure</u> how long it would take to <u>complete</u> the <u>task</u> of making the needle.

Sentence Forms

These two sentences have the same meaning but different forms. In each sentence something is said. The first form, which uses quotation marks, is *direct*. The second form is *indirect*. What differences do you see in the tenses and pronouns in the two forms?

 a. The man's neighbors said, "We are surprised."

 b. The man's neighbors said that they were surprised.

Read each of the following "a." sentences. Then complete the "b." sentences to express the same meaning in indirect speech.

 1. a. The old man answered, "I want to make a needle."

  b. The old man answered that _____.

 2. a. Then he said, "I don't know how long it will take."

  b. Then he said that _____.

 3. He also told his neighbor, "If I die before the job is completed, I will leave the work for my son."

  b. He also told his neighbor that _____

Sentence Combining

Combine each pair of sentences to make a longer sentence with the same meaning. The first two are done for you.

 1. a. This story is about an old man. He was making a needle.

  b. (who) This story is about an old man who was making a needle.

 2. a. The man had a piece of iron. It was very large.

  b. (which) The man had a piece of iron which was very large.

3. a. The man's answer surprised the neighbors. They had seen him working.

   b. (who) _____

4. a. Tailors are people. They use needles in their work.

   b. (who) _____

5. a. Iron is a metal. It is hard and strong.

   b. (which) _____

6. a. Hammers are tools. They are much bigger than needles.

   b. (that) _____

7. a. A needle is a long, sharp pin. It has a hole to put thread through.

   b. (that) _____

Sounds

Some words are hard to read aloud because some letters are not pronounced the way they look; some letters are not pronounced at all.

For example words ending in -tient, -tion, -tial, or -cial (such as patient, potion, and partial) have endings that are pronounced /shunt/, /shun/, and /shul/. Pronounce the following words:

motion   **nation**   **fiction**   **facial**   **spatial**

Some words contain letters that are not pronounced, such as the w in answer or wrist, or the k in know. K is not pronounced in the kn combination at the beginning of words, and w is not pronounced in the wr combination at the beginning of words. Pronounce the following words:

knot   **knife**   **write**   **wrong**   **wrap**

Questions for Comprehension/ Discussion/Writing

○ A *moral* is a lesson taught by a story. What is the lesson or moral of this story?

○ What did the old man think about persistence? What did the neighbors think about the old man? What do you think? Was he wise or foolish? Why?

○ Tell a story from your country that teaches the importance of persistence.

○ Give an example from your own life—or the life of someone you know—that shows the importance of persistence.

○ Do you think the piece of iron will ever really become a needle? Why or why not?

○ There is an old saying: "You may not be able to finish the task, but that doesn't excuse you from beginning it." What does that mean? How does it relate to this story?

A WISE WISH

Before you start to read

○ Look at the top picture on page 16. Find the mountains and the river. Some clothes are lying beside the river. Do you think they belong to a cowboy, a king, or a soldier? Why?

○ Look at the bottom picture on page 16. Two people are wearing big hats. Do you think they are eating, praying, or farming? Explain why you think so.

○ Have you ever done something good for someone you didn't like because you knew it was the right thing to do?

○ When you are reading, think about the actions of the farmers. Would you have done the same thing in their place?

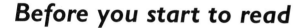

15

1.

2.

A Wise Wish

1   There was once a very bad king. All the people hated him. One hot day the king was walking along the river. He decided to take a swim. The king was a good swimmer, but when he got into the water, he suddenly felt a pain in his side. He started to drown.

2   Two farmers were working in a field nearby. They jumped in the water and saved him. They didn't know that he was the king until he was out of the water.

3   The king was very grateful to the farmers. He said to them, "You have saved my life. Ask me for anything you want." One of the farmers said, "I need two water buffaloes to help me in the fields." The king promised he would give him the animals.

4   Then the king asked the other farmer, "What is your wish." The other farmer was old and wise. He thought and thought. Then he said, "Don't tell anyone that I helped save your life."

Exercises

Word Choice

Choose from the following words to fill in the blanks.

before	drown	grateful	hated
jumped	nearby	promised	

1. The king was far from home, but there was a
   farm _____.

2. The river was deep, and the king couldn't move his
   arms or legs, so he started to _____.

3. He told the farmers who saved him that he was
   very _____.

4. He was glad that they had _____ into the
   water to save him.

5. When he _____ to do something, he
   always did it.

Fill in the blank with the correct verb.

     There was once a very bad king. All the people
h_____ him. One day the king was walking along the
river. He d_____ to take a swim. The king was a good
swimmer, but he g_____ a pain in his side. He s_____
to drown.

Choose from the following prepositions to fill in the blanks.

by	for	in	to	with

1. The king decided to go _____ a swim.

2. He suddenly felt a pain _____ his side.

3. The king agreed _____ the first farmer's request.

4. The wise old farmer thought _____ a while.

5. He knew the king was unpopular _____ his people.

Choose from the following words to fill in the blanks.

if   **that**   **unless**   **until**   **while**

1. The king felt hot _____ he was taking a walk.

2. He swam _____ he got a pain in his side.

3. He would have drowned _____ the farmers had not rescued him.

4. He knew he would drown _____ the farmers rescued him.

5. The old man said, "Don't tell anyone _____ I saved your life."

Sentence Meanings

Which sentences say something that is *true* according to the story? Which sentences say something *false*.

1. _____ The wise farmer was very glad that he had saved the king.

2. _____ The farmers didn't know how to swim.

3. _____ The king didn't know how to swim.

4. _____ One farmer asked for two animals.

5. _____ Everyone hated the king.

Which of the following sentences tells what happened first in the story? Copy that sentence in the first blank line. Then put the other sentences into the right order and copy them.

1. The wise man said, "Don't tell anyone."
2. The two farmers saved the king's life.
3. The king was walking along the river.
4. The king got a pain in his side.
5. The first farmer asked for water buffaloes.

1. _____
2. _____
3. _____
4. _____
5. _____

Match the sentences from the first column with sentences in the second column that have almost the same meaning.

1. _____ He was unpopular.   a. He identified himself.
2. _____ He took a walk.   b. They made a request.
3. _____ He said, "I am the king." c. They rescued him.
4. _____ They asked for something. d. People didn't like him.
5. _____ They saved him.   e. He went for a walk.
                                    f. He liked to walk.
                                    g. He was grateful.

Word Meanings

1. Which of the following are people? Circle the words that refer to people.

buffaloes   farmers   fields
kings   rivers   swimmers

2. Three of the following words have the same meaning. Circle those words.

appreciative   **huge**   **grateful**
persistent   **elderly**   **thankful**

3. Three of the following are animals. Circle those three.

buffaloes   **swimmers**   **farmers**
horses   **wishes**   **cows**

Punctuation

Copy these sentences, adding punctuation and changing small letters to capitals as needed.

1. when the farmers saved the king they didnt know who he was

_____

2. the first farmer asked may i have two water buffaloes

_____

Sounds and Spellings

Four words in each group *rhyme*. Circle the one word that does not rhyme. Do not be tricked by the spelling. Pay attention to the *sounds* of the words.

1. to	go	you	do	true
2. brown	down	grown	drown	noun
3. wise	dies	eyes	buys	days
4. bed	bread	paid	said	dead
5. how	know	no	grow	go

Topics for Discussion/Writing

- ○ The title of the story is *A Wise Wish,* but the story tells about two wishes. What were the two? Which was the "wise" wish according to the storyteller? Do you agree or disagree? Why?

- ○ Suppose the story had started with these sentences: There was once a good king. All the people loved him. How would that change have made a difference in the rest of the story? Write a new story to go with this new beginning.

- ○ Many countries have stories about people who unexpectedly have a chance to make wishes. Do you remember any such stories? Write or tell one.

- ○ If you were in the same place as the farmers, would you have saved the king? Why or why not?

- ○ If you had saved the king, what would you wish for?

- ○ Have you ever helped someone when you didn't want to because you knew it was the right thing to do? Tell about it.

A WISE WISH

1   Once there was a very bad king who was unpopular with all his people.

2   One hot day while he was taking a walk by the river, the king decided to go for a swim. He was a good swimmer, but when he got in the water, he got a cramp. He started to drown.

3   Two farmers who were working in a field nearby saw him drowning and jumped in to rescue him. The king thanked them and identified himself. He was so grateful that he gave each farmer one wish.

4   The first farmer asked for a pair of water buffaloes. The king gladly agreed to this request. Then the king asked the second man to state his wish.

5   The second farmer, a wise old man, thought for a while. Finally he said, "Do not tell anyone that I helped to save your life."

Exercises

Sentence Forms

Combine each pair of sentences using *so. . . that* to make one sentence with the same meaning. Notice that *so* replaces *very* in the combined sentence. The first one is done for you.

1. a. Each story is very short. We can read it again.

   b. The story is so short that we can read it again.

2. a. The king was very bad. All the people hated him.

   b. _____

3. a. The king felt very hot. He decided to take a swim.

   b. _____

4. a. The king was very grateful. He gave each farmer a wish.

   b. _____

5. a. The second farmer was very wise. He thought for a while before he replied.

   b. _____

Word Meanings

Match the words in the first column with their definitions in the second column.

1. _____ unpopular   a. began

2. _____ a request   b. something asked for

3. _____ rescue   c. sometimes

4. _____ field   d. not liked

5.	_____	finally	e. at last
6.	_____	started	f. quick, sharp pain
7.	_____	cramp	g. piece of land for farming
8.	_____	nearby	h. save
9.	_____	hated	i. not far away
10.	_____	sudden	j. happening quickly and unexpectedly
			k. stated as fact
			l. near a mountain
			m. disliked very much

Word Forms

Prefixes and Suffixes Sometimes letters can be added to the beginning of a word (prefix) to change the words meaning. Sometimes letters can be added to the end of a word to change the meaning or the grammatical form.

The prefix *un-* means *not*. It changes a word so it means the opposite.

1. popular   unpopular
2. happy   _____
3. wise   _____

The suffix *-ful* means *full of* or *having a lot of*. The ending makes a word an adjective.

1. help   helpful
2. beauty   _____ (change the y to i)
3. use   _____

The suffix *-ly* usually makes a word an adverb.

1. grateful   gratefully
2. glad   _____
3. lazy   _____ (change the y to i)

Topics for Discussion/Writing

○ Do you swim? What rules of safety do you follow when you swim? Which safety rule didn't the king follow?

○ Do you know what rules you should follow if you see someone drowning? Did the farmers do the right thing? What could they have done instead?

○ Why did the farmers save the king that nobody liked? Why didn't they realize that the man in the water was the king?

THE ANT
AND THE CICADA

Before you start to read

○ Can you think of a time when you didn't prepare for something important?

○ Look at picture #1 on page 28. What are the ants doing? What are the cicadas doing? How is the weather?

○ Look at picture #5 on page 30. What are the ants doing? What are the cicadas doing? How is the weather?

○ Look at picture #7 on page 30. Describe the cicadas. What do you think happened to them?

○ When you read the story, think about the behavior of the ants and the cicadas. Were the ants right when they wouldn't give food to the cicadas? Why?

1.

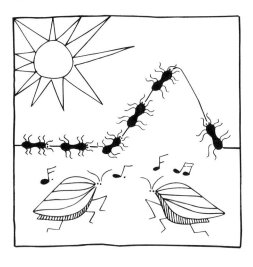

2.

3.

4.

THE ANT
AND THE CICADA

1   In the old days, ants and cicadas were friends. They were very different. The ants were hardworking, but the cicadas were lazy.

2   In the summer, the ant families were very busy. They knew that in the winter they would have to stay in their anthill. They wanted to have enough food for the whole winter.

3   While the ants worked hard, the cicadas didn't do anything. They sang and danced all day. When they were hungry, they could fly to the farm and get something to eat.

4   One day the cicadas were singing and dancing, They saw a long line of ants bringing food to their anthill. The cicadas said, "Stop, my silly friends. It's a very nice day. Come and dance with us." The ants said, "Don't you know about winter? If you don't work now, you'll have trouble later."

5   But the cicadas said, "We have strong wings. We can fly anywhere we want. Stupid ants!" And they continued to sing and dance.

6   In the winter, it rained or snowed all the time, and it was very cold. In the anthill, there was singing and dancing. But the cicadas had nothing to eat. They asked the ants for some food. The ants said, "We thought you could fly anywhere. Now who is stupid and silly?"

7   The cicadas cried and said that their wings were wet from the rain. The ants said, "We're sorry, but now it's too late. If we help you, there won't be enough food for us. Sorry, very sorry." And the ants closed their door.

8   The next day, when the ants opened their door, all the cicadas were dead! That's why we can hear cicadas sing in the summer, but in the winter they are silent.

5.

6.

7.

Exercises

Comprehension

1. In the old days, the ant and the cicada were friends. The ant was *industrious*, but the cicada was lazy. Find a word in paragraph 1 that means the same as industrious.

2. Read paragraph 3 to find out where the cicadas ate in the summer. Read paragraph 7 to find out why they couldn't eat in the same place in the winter.

3. Who sang and danced in the summer?

4. Who sang and danced in the winter?

5. Why did the ants work so hard in the summer?

6. Why didn't the cicadas work hard in the summer?

7. What happened to the cicadas in the winter?

8. Why didn't the cicadas fly away in the winter?

9. How did the ants get ready for the winter?

10. Why didn't the ants give food to the cicadas?

11. "If you don't work hard now, you'll have trouble later." In these sentence above, who was talking? To whom were they talking? What trouble would come later?

Fill in the Blank

In the following sentence, fill in the blanks with verbs from the story.

In the summer, the ant families _____ very busy. They

_____ that in the winter they _____ have to stay in

their anthill. They _____ to have enough food for the

whole winter.

Pronoun Reference

In each sentence, tell who the underlined pronoun is talking about.

1. "<u>They</u> were very different." (paragraph 1)
2. "<u>They</u> worked to have enough food." (paragraph 2)
3. "<u>They</u> sang and danced." (paragraph 3)
4. "<u>We</u> have strong wings." (paragraph 5).
5. "<u>We</u> thought you could fly anywhere." (paragraph 6)

Sentence Structure

Expressions that describe the weather often begin with *it is*. Sometimes the expression ends with an adjective.

Example: It is sunny. It is cold. It is windy.

Other times <u>it</u> is followed by the present progressive tense.

Example: It is raining. It is snowing.

1. Look at picture #1 at the beginning of the story. Describe the weather in that picture.
2. Look at picture #5. Describe the weather in that picture.
3. Describe the weather today.

Vocabulary

Choose from the following words to fill in the blanks. Sometimes two different words might fit.

borrow	different	easy	hardworking	silly
helpless	silent	tired	quiet	

1. I don't have enough sugar for this cake. Can I _____ some from you?

2. During a test, students should be _____.

3. Ron and Bill look _____ even though they are twins.

4. _____ students usually do well in school.

5. When winter came, the cicadas were _____.

True–False

1. _____ The ants worked hard in the winter.

2. _____ Cicadas like to sing and dance.

3. _____ Cicadas can fly.

4. _____ The cicadas flew south for the winter.

5. _____ Ants are hardworking.

6. _____ Ants don't like to sing and dance.

7. _____ The ants shared their food with the cicadas.

8. _____ An anthill is an ant's home.

9. _____ Cicadas don't sing in the winter.

10. _____ The cicadas were hardworking.

Sentence Combining

Use the word *but* to combine sentences when there is a contrast (difference) between the information in the first half of the sentence and the information in the second half of the sentence. The first two are done for you.

1. a. The ants were hardworking. The cicadas were lazy.

   b. The ants were hardworking, but the cicadas were lazy.

2. a. The ants worked in the summer. The cicadas sang and danced.

   b. The ants worked in the summer, but the cicadas sang and danced.

3. a. The ants were happy in the winter. The cicadas were cold and wet.

   b. _____

4. a. Cicadas can fly. Ants crawl.

   b. _____

5. a. The ants had food in the winter. The cicadas didn't.

   b. _____

6. a. Ants and cicadas are insects. Dogs are mammals.

   b. _____

7. a. The winter was cold. The summer was hot.

   b. _____

The Ant and the Cicada

1   Long ago ants and cicadas were friends. The ants were very industrious, but the cicadas were lazy.

B

2   During the summertime, the ants were busy preparing for winter when they would have to stay in all the time.

3   One day when the cicadas were singing and dancing, they saw a long line of ants carrying food to their anthill. The cicadas invited the ants to join them. But the ants said," We have to get ready for the winter. If you don't do the same thing, you'll be sorry later!"

4   The cicadas answered, "We can fly anywhere we want with our strong wings. Stupid ants!" And the cicadas kept on singing and dancing.

5   When the winter came, it was chilly and damp all the time. Inside the anthill, the ants sang and danced. But the cicadas were hungry. They asked the ants if they could borrow some food. The ants said, "We thought you could fly anywhere you wanted!"

6   But the cicadas' wings were wet from the rain and snow. The ants said, "We're sorry. If you had told us, we would have worked harder and saved some food for you, but now it is too late. If we lend you food, there will not be enough food for us. Sorry, very sorry." Then they closed their door.

7   The next day, when the ants opened their door, they found the cicadas dead. That's why, nowadays, we can hear cicadas sing in the summer, but not in the winter.

Exercises B

Vocabulary

Match the words that mean the same(synonyms).

1. _____ hardworking   a. in modern times
2. _____ cold   b. chilly
3. _____ invite   c. having no sound
4. _____ silent   d. ask someone to
                                 go somewhere or
                                 do something

5. _____ prepare   e. get ready
6. _____ nowadays   f. winter

                              h. industrious

Match the words that mean the opposite (antonyms).

1. _____ lend   a. sick
2. _____ winter   b. wet
3. _____ industrious   c. summer
4. _____ dead   d. borrow
5. _____ damp   e. lazy

                              f. alive

                              g. give

                              h. dry

Comprehension

1. "If you don't do the same thing, you'll be sorry later!" What do the ants want the cicadas to do?
2. "We can hear the cicadas sing in the summer, but not in the winter." What doesn't happen in the winter?
3. "Now it is too late." What is it too late for?
4. "If you had told us, we would have worked harder." What should the cicadas have told the ants?

Sentence Combining

Use the word *when* to combine sentences when a specific time,—day, week, season, etc.—is mentioned. Use *where* to combine when a specific place is mentioned. Be sure to place the *when-clause* after the time word and to put the *where-clause* after the place word.

> **Examples:** The ants prepared for the winter. They would have to stay inside then.
>
> The ants prepared for the winter when they would have to stay inside. (Notice the word *then* is not used in the combined sentence).
>
> The ants stayed in the anthill. It was dry there.
>
> The ants stayed in the anthill where it was dry. (Notice that the word *there* is not used in the combined sentence).

Combine the following sentences. Put the *when-cl*... or *where-clause* after the underlined word.

1. a. My favorite season is the <u>summer</u> warm then.

   b. (when) _____

2. a. The <u>winter</u> is a bad time for ... It is cold and wet,

   b. (when) _____

37

T|

3. a. The cicadas flew to the <u>farm</u>. The food was good there.

   b. (where) _____

4. a. The cicadas played <u>outside</u>. It was warm there.

   b. (where) _____

5. a. The cicadas came to the <u>anthill</u>. The ants lived there.

   b. (where) _____

With a partner, write three true sentences that are combined with
when or *where*.

_____

_____

_____

Idiom Practice

Keep on and *go on* mean *continue* or *persist*. They are followed by the
ing form (gerund).

> Example: I fed the baby, but he kept on crying.
>
> The ants told the cicadas to prepare for the winter, but
> they went on singing and dancing.
>
> I have tried to keep the dog in my yard, but he keeps on
> getting out.

○ What is something that your brothers or sisters keep on doing
that you don't like?

○ What is something that you go on doing even when you don't
want to?

○ Name something that you are glad you kept on doing.

○ Is there something that you are sorry that you kept on doing?

and the Cicada

Get ready means *prepare*. When it is followed by a verb, the verb is in the infinitive (to) form.

> **Examples:** The ants got ready to eat in the winter.

- ○ What did you get ready to do this morning?
- ○ How are you getting ready to find a good job?
- ○ What should children get ready to do every morning?
- ○ What should children get ready to do at night?

Sound and Spelling

The letter "C" has two different sounds in the word *cicada*. It also has two different sounds in the words *circle*, *circus*, and *circumference*.
"C" + "I" or "E" is pronounced "S."
"C" + "A", "O", "U," or consonant is pronounced "K."

1. Think of five words in which "C" is pronounced as "S."
2. Think of five words in which "C" is pronounced as "K."
3. Can you think of any other words that contain both pronunciations of "C?"

Prefixes and Suffixes

The ending -*ous* is an adjective ending that means *full of* or *having a lot of*.

> **Examples:** industry—industrious (Note that for words ending in "y" *preceded by a consonant*, "y" becomes "I" before adding "ous.")
> joy—joyous
> marvel—marvelous

How many examples can you find of adjectives with the "ous" ending?

Topics for Discussion/Writing

○ Do you think the ants should have given food to the cicadas? Why or why not?

○ There is a saying in English: "Make hay while the sun shines." It means do work outside (this expression especially refers to work on a farm) while the weather is good. What does that saying have to do with this story?

○ Some stories like this one are written to teach a lesson (or moral). What do you think the lesson is?

○ Some stories are written to explain some fact about nature. What do you learn from this story about when you can hear cicadas and when you can't hear them?

○ Tell another story you know that teaches a lesson similar to this one.

○ Tell about a time when you had trouble because you didn't prepare for something important.

SEÑOR BILLY GOAT

Before you start to read

○ Look at the picture of the vegetable garden on page 42. Which of these vegetables do you know? Which have you eaten? Which are popular in your country?

○ Stop reading after paragraph 4. Can you guess how a little ant could chase away a big goat? Then continue reading to see if you were right.

○ Señor is a Spanish word that means "mister." It is pronounced *senyour*.

42   Señor Billy Goat

Señor Billy Goat

1   Once upon a time a little old man and a little old woman lived in the hills of Puerto Rico. In their garden, they grew many vegetables, such as tomatoes, pumpkins, potatoes, beans, and corn. They spent many hours working in the garden.

2   Every morning while the wife made coffee, the old man looked out the window at his beautiful garden. But one day he saw something in the garden. "Maria, come quickly," he called to his wife. "Something is eating our vegetables."

3   He went out to the garden and saw that it was a billy goat. "Please don't eat up the garden, Mr. Billy Goat! We are old and we need our vegetables," he said. But the goat turned his horns toward the old man and made him run away.

4   The old man and his wife started to cry. Just then a little black ant fell into the man's hand. "What will you give me if I help you?" asked the ant. "I can make the goat go away." They promised her a little bag of flour and a little bag of sugar, and she went away.

5   The ant went to the garden. She walked up the goat's leg, over his back, and up to his ear. Then she stung him.

"Ouch," cried the goat. The ant began to sting the goat on his ears, legs, and back.

6   "I must have stepped on an anthill!" the billy goat said, and he ran out of the garden. He rolled on the ground to try to kill the ant. But he forgot that he was on a hill. So he rolled down, down, down. Maybe he is still rolling!

7   The man and his wife were happy. They gave the ant a bag of flour and one of sugar, as they had promised. After that, they never had problems with goats.

Exercises

Sentence Completion

Choose from the following words to fill in the blanks.

angry	ant	asked	garden	horns
make	spoke	quickly	sold	pumpkins
spends	still	promised	stung	thought
turned	toward			

1. The goat pushed the old man with its _____.

2. The old man and the old woman _____ to give flour and sugar to the ant.

3. From their _____ , they got food to eat and sell.

4. The goat _____ that he had stepped on an anthill.

5. They grew _____ in their garden.

6. A bee _____ the boy on his arm.

7. I have looked for the book for two weeks, but I _____ haven't found it.

8. They answered the old man when he _____ to them.

9. Maria added more oil to _____ the machine run better.

10. The father was _____ when the child came home late.

Sequencing

Put these sentences in the correct order. For example, write **1** next to the sentence that tells what happened first.

_____ The man and his wife started to cry.

_____ The goat rolled down, down, down.

_____ The old man saw something in his garden.

_____ The ant stung the goat.

_____ The old man asked the goat not to eat the vegetables in the garden.

_____ The ant said that she could make the goat go away.

True–False

1. _____ The old man was unhappy to see the goat.

2. _____ The billy goat saw the ant coming.

3. _____ The goat wasn't hungry.

4. _____ The old man paid the ant for her help.

5. _____ At first the old man tried to talk to the goat.

Word Groups

Circle the word in each column that does not belong.

A	B	C
chicken	apples	roll
goat	potatoes	fall
pumpkin	corn	grow
cicada	beans	ask
	spinach	spend
		down

Reading from Context

> Once upon a time, a little old man and a little old woman lived in the *highlands* of Puerto Rico. In their garden, they grew many *crops*.

Look at the first paragraph of "Señor Billy Goat." What word means the same as *highlands*? What are some crops that the old man and woman grew in their garden?

In paragraph 4, find the sentence, "*They* promised *her* a little bag of flour." Who are *they*? Who does *her* refer to?

Talk About

"Once upon a time . . ." is the way many stories begin in English. When we see these words, we know that we are going to read about something that happened a long time ago. We also know that this is not a true story. Many children's stories start with these words. There are also other ways to start a story. Look at the first lines of other stories in this book. What other beginning phrases do you see?

"And they lived happily ever after" is often used to end stories in English. Is there a usual way to begin and end stories in your country?

Capitalization/Punctuation

Rewrite the following sentences using proper capitalization and punctuation.

1. please dont eat up the garden mr billy goat we are old and we need our vegetables he said

    _____

2. what will you give me if i help you asked the ant i can make the goat go away

    _____

3. maria come quickly he called something is eating our vegetables

    _____

Topics for Discussion/Writing

○ Ants were used in two stories, "The Ant and the Cicada" and "Señor Billy Goat." From these two stories, what do you know about ants?

○ In this story, a very small animal outsmarts a much larger, stronger animal. Can you think of similar stories with

a. a younger brother and an older brother?

b. a young boy and a giant?

c. a poor young girl and her rich older sisters?

d. a smart, small animal and a big powerful animal?

○ Can you think of other stories in which an animal helps people?

○ Now that you have read this story, tell what crops grow in Puerto Rico. What crops grow in your native country?

Señor Billy Goat

1   Once upon a time, an old couple lived in the highlands of Puerto Rico. They had a garden where they grew many crops, such as tomatoes, pumpkins, potatoes, beans, and corn.

2   Every morning while his wife prepared the coffee, the old man looked out the window at his beautiful garden. One day, the man thought he saw something digging in his garden. He went outside to check, and sure enough, there was a billy goat in the garden. He begged the billy goat to go away, but the goat refused to leave.

3   The old couple began to cry, but a little ant came and offered to help them in exchange for one tiny sack of flour and one of sugar.

4   The ant went to the garden and started to crawl all over the billy goat. "Ouch!" cried the goat, as the little ant stung him. "I must have stepped on an anthill!" he cried, running out of the garden.

5   He tried to get rid of the ant by rolling on the ground. But he forgot that he was on a hill, so he rolled down, down, down. Perhaps he's still rolling.

6   Of course the old man and the old woman were happy. They gave flour and sugar to the ant as they had promised. They never saw the billy goat again. And they lived happily ever after.

Exercises

Matching

Match the words in the first column with their definitions in the second column.

1. _____ prepare

2. _____ refused

3. _____ sack

4. _____ get rid of

5. _____ begged

6. _____ crawl

7. _____ exchange

8. _____ tiny

9. _____ couple

10. _____ crops

11. _____ highlands

12. _____ sure enough

13. _____ sting

14. _____ roll

15. _____ perhaps

a. hills

b. cried

c. wake up

d. plants we grow to eat or use

e. said "no"

f. really, certainly

g. trade one thing for another

h. help

i. bag

j. move on hands and knees

k. stayed

m. make go away

n. asked for

o. very little

p. husband and wife

q. get ready

r. maybe

s. fall over and over

t. an insect bite

Matching Phrases

Write the letter of the phrase in column B that goes with the phrase in column A.

A	B
1. _____ Ouch	a. I probably saw it.
2. _____ They got rid of it.	b. It turned over and over.
3. _____ It arrives every morning	c. I refused to do it.
4. _____ I gave it in exchange.	d. Oh, it hurts.
5. _____ It rolled down the street.	e. It comes daily.
6. _____ I must have seen it.	f. It's possible.
	g. It was traded for another one.
	h. They made it go away.

Punctuation

Copy these sentences, adding punctuation and changing small letters to capital letters as needed.

1. maria come quickly he called to his wife something is eating our vegetables

   _____

2. then she stung him ouch cried the goat

   _____

3. i must have stepped on an anthill the billy goat said and he ran out of the garden

   _____

Dictionary Work

The following words have more than one meaning. Use your dictionary to define the underlined word the way it is used in the sentence. Also tell its grammatical function in the sentence.

1. They grew many <u>crops</u> in their garden.

    definition _____

    part of speech _____

2. They gave the ant a <u>sack</u> of flour.

    definition _____

    part of speech _____

3. The goat <u>rolled</u> on the ground.

    definition _____

    part of speech _____

4. The goat rolled on the <u>ground</u>.

    definition _____

    part of speech _____

5. The old man went outside to <u>check</u>.

    definition _____

    part of speech _____

Pronoun Reference

1. They gave the ant one sack of sugar and *one* of flour.

    One means _____

2. The old couple began to cry, but a little ant said that *she* would help *them*.

    She means _____

    Them means _____

Sentence Combining

Combine each pair of sentences, using the word *one*, to make one sentence with the same meaning. The first one is done for you.

1. a. He gave her a sack of flour. He gave her a sack of sugar.

   b. <u>He have her a sack of flour and one of sugar.</u>

2. a. Sally gave him a box of cereal. She gave him a box of cookies.

   b. _____

3. a. Mike brought three cans of blue paint. He bought one can of red paint.

   b. _____

4. a. Please get two quarts of orange juice. Get one quart of milk.

   b. _____

Combine the following sentences using the "-ing" form. The first one is done for you.

1. a. He saw the goat. It was digging in the garden.

   b. <u>He saw the goat digging in the garden.</u>

2. a. She heard her husband. He was calling her.

   b. _____

3 a. The cicadas saw the ants. They were carrying food.

   b. _____

4 a. The girl saw an old man. He was sharpening a piece of iron.

   b. _____

Sentence Structure

We use the phrase *must have* when something is certain or probable: "I *must have* stepped on an anthill." The negative form of *must have* is *can't have*. Use *must have* or *can't have* in the following sentences.

1. They _____ come yet; it's too soon.

2. I don't see Don, so he _____ left.

3. Alice can't find the car keys. She _____ left them somewhere.

4. The library _____ closed; the lights are out.

5. The park is twenty miles away; they _____ walked here in half an hour.

Point of View

Re-tell this story from the ant's point of view. The first sentence is written for you.

> One day I met an old couple who were crying in their garden . . .

Tell the story from the old man's point of view.

> One day I was looking out at my garden . . .

Topics for Discussion/Writing

○ *Get rid of* means make something go away. Did you ever have pests (annoying animals or insects) in your house? How did you get rid of them?

○ If you were the old man, what would you do to get rid of the goat?

THE MOUNTAIN GOD AND THE RIVER GOD

Before you start to read

○ Look at the picture on page 56. Who is this woman? How do you know?

○ Where is she? Read the story to find out why she is there.

○ What natural event is explained by this story?

○ In your opinion, what is the best way to find someone to marry? As you read the story, think about the way the king chose a husband for his daughter.

The Mountain God and the River God

THE MOUNTAIN GOD AND THE RIVER GOD

1   A long time ago in Vietnam, there was a beautiful princess. She was the king's only daughter.

2   Both the mountain god and the river god wanted to marry the king's daughter. The king said, "You must fight, and the winner will marry the princess."

3   So the two gods fought. They fought with bows and arrows. The mountain god won the fight, and he married the beautiful princess.

4   But the river god was angry. He used his power to attack the mountain. The river got higher. It covered the mountain. It came up to where the mountain god and the princess lived. Then the mountain god used his power. The mountain got higher too, so the river couldn't get the princess.

5   Now every year in July and August, when the rains come in Vietnam and the rivers rise, people say that the river god is still trying to take away the princess.

Exercises

True–False

1. _____ The king married the mountain god.

2. _____ The princess married the mountain god.

3. _____ The two gods fought with guns.

4. _____ The mountain god won the fight.

5. _____ The rivers in Vietnam rise in July and August.

6. _____ The river god was angry after the fight.

7. _____ Both gods wanted to marry the princess.

8. _____ The mountain got higher.

9. _____ The river got so high that it got the princess.

10. _____ The princess was the king's only daughter.

Vocabulary

Choose from the following words to fill in the blanks:

attack	**bow and arrow**	**rise**	**power**
river	**mountain**	**princess**	

1. The daughter of a king is a _____.

2. A very high hill is called a _____.

3. The hunter used a _____ to kill animals.

4. The mountain god was very strong. He had a lot of

   _____.

5. Soldiers sometimes _____ their enemies.

Sentence Order

Put these sentences in the correct order.

1. _____ The river god was angry.

2. _____ The two gods wanted to marry the princess.

3. _____ The river got higher.

4. _____ The mountain god won the fight.

5. _____ The mountain got higher.

Comprehension

1. Where did this story take place?

2. Which god won the fight?

3. What weapon (tool for fighting) did the gods use?

4. What natural event does this story explain?

5. Who decided which god the princess would marry? How was this decided?

Sounds and Spellings

gh

○ Sometimes *gh* is silent, as in *fought, caught,* or *taught.* Can you think of other words in which *gh* is silent?

○ Sometimes *gh* sounds like *f,* as in *tough, laugh,* or *rough.* In what other words does *gh* sound like *f?*

ow

○ Sometimes *ow* sounds like *o* as in *bow* (meaning weapon or hair ribbon) or *tow.* Can you think of other words in which *ow* is pronounced *o?*

○ Sometimes *ow* is pronounced *ow* as in bow (bend at the waist), *flower,* or *cow.* Can you think of other words in which *ow* sounds like *ow?*

Pronoun References

Tell who the underlined pronouns represent.

"The mountain god and the river god came to the king to ask if they could marry her."

"He used his power to attack the mountain." (paragraph 4)

"It covered the mountain." (paragraph 4)

Sentence Combining

Follow the instructions to combine the following pairs of sentences.

1 a. The two gods fought. They fought with bows and arrows.

     b. (take out two words) _____

2 a. The river god was angry. He used his power to attack the mountain.

     b. (so) _____

3 a. The river god was angry. He used his power to attack the mountain. _____

     b. (so . . .that)_____

4 a. The river got higher. It covered the mountain.

     b. (until)_____

5 a. There was a beautiful princess. She was the king's only daughter.

     b. (who) _____

THE MOUNTAIN GOD AND THE RIVER GOD

1   Once upon a time in the days of King Hung Vuong in Vietnam, there was a beautiful princess. She was the king's only daughter.

2   Both the river god and the mountain god came to the king. Each wanted to ask for the hand of the king's only daughter. But the king told them that they first had to fight each other, and the winner could marry the princess.

3   So the two gods had a contest with bows and arrows. The mountain god won, and he married the beautiful princess.

4   But the river god was angry. He attacked the mountain with all his might. He made the river rise and flow around the mountain. Soon it had almost reached the princess! In response, the mountain rose, too, so the water couldn't reach the princess.

5   That was many years ago. But even today, in July and August when the rains come in Vietnam and the rivers rise, people remember the rivalry between the two gods. The people say that the river god is still trying to take away the princess.

Exercises

Matching

Match the word in the first column with the words in the second column that mean the opposite (antonyms).

1. _____ angry
2. _____ rivalry
3. _____ daughter
4. _____ king
5. _____ remember
6. _____ winner
7. _____ rose

a. fell
b. friendship
c. forget
d. happy
e. loser
f. man
g. queen
h. question
i. son
j. unhappy

Synonyms

Three of the words or phrases in each group mean almost the same thing. Circle the word or phrase that is different.

1. might   power   strength   persistence

2. rivalry   friendship   competition   contest

3. rise   go up   get higher   respond

4. in response to in spite of   as a result of as a reaction to

Word Choice

Choose from the following words or phrases to fill in the blanks:

all his might   **contest**   **attacked**   **flowed**   **left**
bow and arrow   **rivalry**   **to prepare**   **reached**   **marry**
to ask for the hand of

1. In the past when a man wanted to marry a woman, he went to her father _____ his daughter.

2. They had a _____ to decide who was the better fighter.

3. After a heavy rain, the river _____ over its banks.

4. The two teams competed; there was a _____ between them.

5. The fighter _____ his enemy using a _____ as a weapon.

Word Forms

Choose from the following word forms to fill in the blanks.

arose   **raise**   **rise**   **risen**
rises   **rising**   **rose**

1. Every summer the river _____.

2. The water in the lake is _____ because of the rain.

3. The water _____ so high that it caused flooding.

Dictionary Use

Each of the following words has more than one meaning. Use your dictionary to find the best definition for the underlined word as it is used in each sentence.

1. She put a yellow <u>bow</u> in her hair.

   definition _____

   part of speech _____ pronunciation _____

2. The hunter shot the animal with a <u>bow</u> and arrow.

   definition _____

   part of speech _____ pronunciation _____

3. The man had to <u>bow</u> when the king passed by.

   definition _____

   part of speech _____ pronunciation _____

4. The gods fought with all their <u>might</u>.

   definition _____

   part of speech _____ pronunciation _____

5. If the river gets high enough, the princess <u>might</u> drown.

   definition _____

   part of speech _____ pronunciation _____

6. The water level <u>rose</u> dangerously.

   definition _____

   part of speech _____ pronunciation _____

7. The prince bought the princess a <u>rose</u>.

   definition _____

   part of speech _____ pronunciation _____

8. She wore a <u>rose</u>-colored dress.

definition _____

part of speech _____ pronunciation _____

9. The mountain god won the <u>contest</u>.

definition _____

part of speech _____ pronunciation _____

10. The river god wanted to <u>contest</u> the results of the competition.

definition _____

part of speech _____ pronunciation _____

Idiom and Phrase Usage

1. Which words in paragraph 2 means *ask to marry*?

_____

2. Which word in paragraph 3 means *competition*?

_____

3. Which word in paragraph 4 means *power*?

_____

4. Which word in paragraph 5 means *serious* (perhaps unfriendly)

competition? _____

Sentence Combining

Combine the following sentences using *both . . . and*. The first one is done for you.

1. a. The river god wanted to marry the princess. The mountain god wanted to marry the princess.

   b. <u>Both the river god and the mountain god wanted to marry the princess.</u>

2. a. The river god had magic powers. The mountain god had magic powers.

   b. _____

3. a. The river got higher. The mountain got higher.

   b. _____

Topics for Discussion/Writing

○ Who decided whom the princess would marry? How was it decided? Would you want to marry someone chosen for you in this way? Why or why not?

○ Discuss the behavior of the river god. What did he do? Why did he do it? Would you have acted in the same way in his place? Why or why not?

○ In your opinion, is it better to choose your own spouse (husband or wife) or have your parents choose one for you? What are the good points and the problems of choosing your own spouse? Of having your parents choose for you?

○ Tell a story that explains the reason for heavy rains, floods, snow, etc.

THE WIND AND THE SUN

Before you start to read

○ Which do you think is more powerful, sun or wind? Which can do more damage to people and animals? to crops? to property?

○ Would it be worse for you to be out on a very windy day or on a very sunny day? Why?

○ What are the benefits of wind, sun, snow, and rain? What harm can they do?

1.

2.

THE WIND AND THE SUN

1   One day the wind started an argument with the sun. "I am stronger than you are!" said the wind. "No," answered the sun, "I am much stronger than you are."

A   While they were talking, they saw a man walking down the road. He was wearing a heavy coat. The sun said to the wind, "Now let us see which of us can make the man take off his coat. Then we will know who is stronger."

2   First the wind tried. It began to blow very hard. It blew so hard that the man pulled the coat around him. The wind was angry at the man. Then the wind said to the sun, "Now it's your turn. Let's see if you can make the man take off his coat!"

3   The sun began to shine down on the man. Soon it got very hot! The man took off his coat. The argument was over.

Exercises

Word Forms

Choose from the following words to fill in the blanks.

strong   **stronger**   **strongest**   **strongly**

1. The sun shone _____.

2. The sun was _____ than the wind.

3. The first man lifted 200 pounds. He is very _____.

4. The second man lifted 250 pounds. He is _____ than the first man.

5. The third man lifted 300 pounds. He is the _____ of all.

Dictionary Skills

For the underlined words, write the dictionary definition that fits their usage in the sentence.

1. The wind tried to <u>blow</u> as hard as it could.

   definition _____

2. The man was knocked out by a <u>blow</u> to the head.

   definition _____

3. The wind said, "Now it's your <u>turn</u>."

   definition _____

4. The man <u>turned</u> away from the wind.

   definition _____

5. The man <u>took off</u> his jacket.

definition _____

6. The airplane <u>took off</u> on time.

definition _____

Irregular Verbs

Write the *irregular* past tense form for the following verbs from the story.

Present tense	Past Tense
blow	_____
take	_____
shine	_____
say	_____
is	_____
make	_____
begin	_____
get	_____
see	_____

Write down all the *regular* past tense forms in this story.

1. _____
2. _____
3. _____
4. _____

Comprehension

1. "First the wind tried." (paragraph 3). What did the wind try to do?
2. "The argument was over" (paragraph 4). What was the argument about? Who won the argument? How do you know?
3. How did the sun make the man take off his coat?
4. Why was the wind angry?

True–False

1. _____ The wind blew the man's coat off.
2. _____ The sun won the argument.
3. _____ The wind was angry with the man.
4. _____ The sun started an argument with the wind.
5. _____ The man was wearing a light coat.

Put these sentences in the correct order.

1. _____ The man pulled his coat tightly around him.
2. _____ The wind said, "I am stronger than you are."
3. _____ The wind blew hard.
4. _____ The man took off his coat.
5. _____ The sun began to shine on the man.

Retelling the Story

Look at the pictures on page 68. Retell the story in your own words.

THE WIND AND THE SUN

1   One day the wind, who loved to argue, said to the sun, "I am stronger than you." But the sun disagreed. "No, you're not," he answered. "I am much more powerful than you."

2   As they were talking, they saw a man walking along the road toward them. He had on a heavy coat. The sun turned toward the wind and suggested that they see who could make the man take off his coat. "That way," the sun said, "we will know which of us is stronger."

3   The wind tried first. It blew harder and harder. Finally, it blew so hard that the man shivered and pulled the coat tightly around him. The wind was angry. It waited to see what the sun would do.

4   Then the sun shone down on the man. Soon the man felt so hot that he took off his coat. That was the end of the argument.

Exercises

Vocabulary

Choose from the following words to fill in the blanks.

angry	argument	blew	disagreed
heavy	looked	shivered	suggested
tightly	turned to	waited	

1. The man _____ because of the cold.

2. The sun and wind _____ about who was stronger.

3. Even though his coat was _____, the man was cold.

4. I _____ my sister and said "Let's go out."

5. The child held his mother's hand _____.

Word Form

Choose from the following word forms to fill in the blanks.

argue	argument	argued	argues	arguing

1. The wind loved to _____.

2. He had an _____ with the sun.

3. The sun and the wind were _____ about who was stronger.

Sentence Combining

Use the word in parentheses to combine each pair of sentences into one sentence.

1. a. The wind loved to argue. The wind said, "I am stronger than you."

   b. (who) _____

2. a. They were walking. They saw a man.

   b. (as) _____

3. a. The man felt hot. He took off his coat.

   b. (so . . . that) _____

4. a. The wind blew hard. The man pulled his coat around him.

   b. (so . . .that) _____

Pronoun Reference

Write the noun that each italicized pronoun refers to.

1. *It* blew so hard that the man pulled his coat around *him*."

   (paragraph 3)   it: _____   him: _____

2. *You* know that . . . I am stronger than *you*."

   (paragraph 1)   you: _____   I: _____

Prefixes

dis- means negation or rejection. It often means not. What is the meaning of the following words?

agree	**disagree**
approve	**disapprove**
appear	**disappear**

Use your dictionary to find three other words in which *dis-* is used with a negative meaning.

Modified Cloze Exercise

One day the wind, who loved to argue, said to the sun, "You know that I am s_____ than you." But the sun d_____. "No, you're not," he a_____. "I am much stronger than you are!"

The wind t_____ first. It blew harder and harder. Finally, it b_____ so hard that the man s_____ and p_____ the coat tightly around him. The wind was angry. It w_____ to see what the sun would do. Then the sun s_____ down on the man. Soon the man f_____ so hot that he _____ off his coat.

Choose the best title for the story. Explain your choice.
- ◯ Why the Wind Blows
- ◯ Why the Sun Shines
- ◯ How the Sun Proved His Strength
- ◯ The Man and His Heavy Coat

Retelling the Story

Pretend that *the sun* is telling this story. Begin with this sentence:

One day the wind, who always liked to argue, said to me, "You know that I am stronger than you."

Topics for Discussion/ Writing

- ◯ Discuss a time when wind or sun hurt someone or something.
- ◯ Did you ever win an argument with actions rather than words? Write or tell about it.
- ◯ Do you know another story about the wind or the sun? Tell it.

THE GOLDEN TOUCH

Before you start to read

○ Did you ever wish for something and then find that you were sorry after you got it?

○ Did you ever wish that you were rich?

○ Stop after paragraph 2. What do you think will happen when the king gets his wish. Will he be glad or sorry? Continue reading to see if you were right.

○ What would be the advantages of having everything you touch turn to gold? What would be the disadvantages?

○ Look at the pictures on page 78. What do you know about the man in the first picture? Who is the little girl?

○ Is the king happy or sad in picture #5? How do you know?

1.

2.

3.

4.

5.

6.

7.

THE GOLDEN TOUCH

1   There once was a king. He was very rich. The king loved two things: his little daughter and his gold. He had many rooms full of gold, but he was not happy. He wanted to have more gold.

2   One day the king was in his garden. A stranger came to see him. The visitor told the king to make a wish. The king said, "I wish to have more gold." "I will help you get your wish," the stranger answered. "Tomorrow morning, everything you touch will change to gold."

3   The next morning the king got up early. He touched a chair, a flower, and a table. Everything changed to gold! The king was very happy. He sat down to eat his breakfast, but his food turned to gold when he touched it. He thought, "If I can't eat anything, I will die."

4   Then his little daughter came into the room. She ran to her father. But when he touched her, she changed to gold, too.

5   The king was very sad. He walked alone in his garden. Then he saw the stranger again. "Oh," cried the king, "please take back my wish. I don't want any more gold." "All right," said the stranger, "if you are really sure this time, I will take back your wish."

6   After that the king was not as rich, but he was wiser and happier.

A

Exercises

Vocabulary

Choose from the following words to fill in the blanks:

change   daughter   gold   king
rich   stranger   touch   wise

1. That can break easily, so please don't _____ it.

2. The man loved his _____ very much, so he was unhappy when she went away.

3. Because he was a _____ in that town, he didn't know where to go.

4. When people grow up, they often _____; they don't stay exactly the same.

5. Benjamin Franklin once said, "Early to bed and early to rise makes a man healthy, wealthy, and _____."

Comprehension

1. What two things did the king love? Which one do you think he loved more? How do you know?
2. Why wasn't the king happy at the beginning of the story?
3. How did the king get "the golden touch"?
4. When did the king first realize that the "golden touch" was a problem?
5. Why wasn't the king happy after he got his wish?
6. Why do you think this story is called "the golden touch."
7. "After that, the king was not as rich, but he was wiser and happier (paragraph 7). What does *after that* refer to?

Sentence Order

Put these sentences in the correct order.

1. _____ The king's daughter turned to gold.
2. _____ The king asked for more gold.
3. _____ The king asked the stranger to take back the wish.
4. _____ A chair turned to gold.
5. _____ The king's food turned to gold.
6. _____ The king was wiser and happier.
7. _____ The stranger said, "Everything you touch will change to gold."

True–False

1. _____ The king was happy because he had so much gold.
2. _____ The king loved gold more than he loved his daughter.
3. _____ If the king had kept "the golden touch" for a long time, he would have died.
4. _____ The king was very happy with "the golden touch."
5. _____ The king didn't want to keep the "golden touch."

Antonyms

Circle the word in each list that means the *opposite* of the first word.

1. **happy**	glad	tired	sad	mean
2. **give**	ask for	lend	take back	want
3. **rich**	money	poor	wealthy	important
4. **wise**	stupid	smart	rude	unhappy
5. **stranger**	visitor	friend	king	daughter

Famous Sayings

The following are famous sayings. Explain how each saying fits this story.

○ Who is rich? He who is satisfied with what he has.
○ Money can't buy happiness.
○ The best things in life are free.
○ Money isn't everything.
○ Beware of what you wish for. You might get it.

Vocabulary from Context

Look at paragraph 1 of the story to guess the meaning of the underlined words.

There once was a <u>monarch</u>. He was very <u>wealthy</u>. He had many rooms full of gold, but he was not <u>satisfied</u>. He wanted to <u>possess</u> more gold.

Synonyms and Antonyms.

1. What word in paragraph 3 means the opposite of *sad* in paragraph 4?
2. What word in paragraph 3 means the same as *turned to* in the same paragraph?

Retelling the Story

Look at the pictures on pages 78-79 and retell the story.

THE GOLDEN TOUCH

1   There once lived a king named Midas who was very rich. He loved two things above all else: his little daughter and his gold. The king had many rooms full of gold, but he wasn't satisfied. He wanted to possess even more gold.

2   One day when the king was in his garden, an unknown visitor came to him. He told the king that he could wish for anything he wanted. At first the king did not believe the stranger, but finally he was convinced. "I wish to have more gold," the king said." Very well," answered the stranger. "You shall have your wish. Beginning tomorrow, everything you touch will turn to gold."

3   The next morning the king got out of bed early. He wanted to see if his wish had been granted. First he touched a chair, then a flower, then a table. Everything he touched turned to gold! The king was very happy. Then he sat down to eat breakfast. But as soon as he touched his food, it turned to gold. The king began to worry. What would happen if he couldn't eat anything?

4   Just then the little princess came into the dining room. She ran to her father. But as he touched her, she turned to gold.

5   The king was sad and worried. He went out to the garden. As he was walking, he saw the stranger again. The king begged him to take back the wish. "I don't want any more gold," he cried. The stranger warned the king to be absolutely sure this time. Then he agreed to take back the wish.

6   From that day on, the king was a wiser and happier man, even though he had less gold.

Exercises

Dictionary Skills

The following underlined words have more than one meaning. Use the dictionary to define each word as it is used in the sentence.

1. Some students need a <u>grant</u> to go to college.

   definition _____

   part of speech _____

2. The Sunshine Foundation <u>grants</u> the wishes of sick children.

   definition _____

   part of speech _____

3. Children shouldn't talk to <u>strangers</u>.

   definition _____

   part of speech _____

4. Sometimes truth is <u>stranger</u> than fiction.

   definition _____

   part of speech _____

Grammar Notes

too and very. Too means excessive, more than is good or acceptable.
Very means much or a lot.
- ○ The king liked gold very much. After he got the "golden touch," he realized that he had liked gold too much.
- ○ She likes her bath water very hot. But if the water is too hot, she could get burned.
- ○ Children like to eat candy very much. But if they eat too much candy, they may get cavities in their teeth.

Put *too* or *very* in the following sentences.

1. John loves his girlfriend _____ much, so he is going to ask her to marry him.

2. Because Jane spends _____ much time with her boyfriend, her grades in school are bad.

3. If people spend _____ much time in the sun, they can get skin cancer.

4. She liked her birthday present _____ much.

Comparative Forms

- ○ Most one or two syllable words add *er* to an adjective to make the comparative form, such as tall–taller, young–younger.
- ○ Words ending in *e* just add *r* to form the comparison. For example, nice–nicer
- ○ Words ending in *y* preceded by a consonant change the *y* to *i* before adding *er*. For example, happy–happier.

Write the comparative form for the following adjectives.

1. wise _____

2. strange _____

3. happy _____

4. rich _____

Matching

Match the words in the first column with their definitions in the second column.

1. _____ above all else
2. _____ absolutely
3. _____ agreed
4. _____ begged
5. _____ beginning
6. _____ convinced
7. _____ dining room
8. _____ from that day on
9. _____ granted
10. _____ just then
11. _____ possess
12. _____ satisfied
13. _____ unknown
14. _____ very well
15. _____ worry
16. _____ warned
17. _____ stranger

a. not sick
b. not smart
c. starting
d. own
e. more than anything
f. after that time
g. happy, content
h. at that time
i. unfamiliar, strange
j. all right, okay
k. given
l. place to eat
m. made to believe
n. asked for, pleaded
o. completely, definitely
p. cautioned
q. said "yes"
r. to be nervous, upset
s. unknown visitor
t. full

Sentence Combining

Use the words in parentheses to combine the sentences.

1 a. There was once a king. He was very rich.

   b. (who) _____

2 a. He had many rooms full of gold. He was not happy.

   b. (but) _____

3 a. He had many rooms full of gold. He was not happy.

   b. (although) _____

4 a. The king was in his garden one day. A stranger came to see him.

   b. (when) _____

5 a. The king was not as rich. He was happier and wiser.

   b. (but) _____

6 a. The king was not as rich. He was happier and wiser.

   b. (Even though) _____

7 a. What would happen to him? He couldn't eat.

   b. (if) _____

8 a. He touched her. She turned to gold.

   b. (as) _____

9 a. He told the king. The king could wish for anything he wanted.

   b. (that) _____

Combine the sentences by reducing the second sentence to an adjective. The first one is done for you.

1 a. There was a king. He was very rich.

   b. There was a very rich rich.

2 a. He had a daughter. She was little.

   b. _____

3 a. The king made a wish. His wish was foolish.

   b. _____

Topics for Discussion/Writing

○ To have the "Midas touch" or "the golden touch" means that a person makes a lot of money in business dealings. Discuss someone you know who has the "Midas touch."

○ How is this story like "The Wise Wish?" How is it different?

○ Tell a story about someone who got what he/she wished for and then was sorry.

○ What do you think the king's life was like after the story?

○ Does this story tell us anything about other people? About ourselves? Is the king like anyone you have ever met?

THE MAGIC BOX

Before you start to read

○ People often tell stories about city people in the country and country people in the city. Why do you think these stories are popular? Do you remember any that you have heard?

○ Look at the pictures on page 92. What do you think is happening in those pictures? Read the story to see if you are right.

○ Stop reading after paragraph 2 and try to guess the end. Then finish reading to see if you guessed correctly.

1.

2.

3.

4.

5.

The Magic Box

THE MAGIC BOX

1   A plain country woman was visiting the city for the first time. She went into a very tall building. On the first floor, she saw an old lady standing in front of a door. The door was closed, and over the door there were lights.

2   Then the door opened. The old lady standing in front of the door went inside. Then it closed. A few minutes later the door opened again, and a beautiful young woman walked out! The country woman thought, "This is the door to a magic box! If I go inside the box, I will be beautiful when I come out."

3   She waited for the door to open again. Then she walked in. But inside the door, she saw a lot of buttons on the wall. And she didn't know what buttons to push!

Exercises

Comprehension

1. You see this "magic box" all the time. You may have one in your school.

   a. What is "the magic box"?
   b. What were the lights over the door?
   c. What were the buttons inside the magic box?
   d. Why didn't the country woman know what it was?

2. Think about the descriptive adjectives used in this story.

   a. Why does the author tell you that the woman was plain?
   b. Why does the author tell you that the woman is a country woman?
   c. Why does the author tell you that the building is tall?

3. Did the country woman become beautiful when she entered the magic box? Why or why not?

Put these sentences in the correct order.

1. _____ The country woman came into a tall building.
2. _____ A beautiful young woman walked out of the magic box.
3. _____ An old woman walked into the magic box.
4. _____ The country woman saw many buttons on the wall.
5. _____ The country woman walked into the magic box.

True–False

1. _____ The box was really a magic box.
2. _____ The woman came from another country.
3. _____ The country woman became young and beautiful.
4. _____ The old woman became young and beautiful.
5. _____ The country woman entered the magic box.

Vocabulary from Context

1. An *unattractive* country woman was visiting the city.

   Look at paragraph 1, sentence 1, to help you guess the meaning of *unattractive* _____

2. She went into a *skyscraper*.

   Look at sentence 1 of paragraph 1 to guess the meaning of *skyscraper* _____

3. The door was *shut*, and over the door there were lights.

   Look at the last sentence of paragraph 1 to help you guess the meaning of *shut*. _____

4. She noticed an *elderly* lady standing in front of a door.

   Look at paragraph 1, sentence 2, to guess the meaning of *elderly* _____

THE MAGIC BOX

1   An unattractive country woman who was visiting the city for the first time entered a skyscraper. On the ground floor, she noticed an old lady standing in front of a door. Over the door there were several lights.

2   As the country woman watched, the door opened and the elderly woman stepped inside. A few minutes later, the door opened again, and out came a beautiful young woman! The country woman was amazed. "This must be the door to a magic box!" she thought. "If I go inside, maybe I, too, will be beautiful when I come out!"

3   She waited for the door to open again. When it did, she eagerly walked in. Then she looked all around. She could see nothing but buttons on the wall, and she had no idea which one to push!

Exercises

Comprehension

1. When *it* did, *she* eagerly walked in.
   a. What is "it?"
   b. Who is she?
   c. When it did . . . Did what?

2. "*She* had no idea which *one* to push."
   a. Who was she?
   b. What does "one" refer to?

3. "She had no idea which one to push!" This means
   a. She didn't have any ideas.
   b. She wanted to push some buttons.
   c. She didn't know which button to push.
   d. She pushed all the buttons.

4. "She could see nothing but buttons . . ." This means
   a. She saw nothing.
   b. She saw only buttons.
   c. She saw buttons and other things.
   d. She couldn't see.

True–False

1. _____ The country woman saw nothing on the wall inside the box.
2. _____ The country woman became beautiful.
3. _____ The country woman thought that the box was magic.
4. _____ There were buttons on the wall inside the box.
5. _____ The box was a magic box.

Matching

1. _____ amazed
2. _____ eagerly
3. _____ entered
4. _____ ground floor
5. _____ had no idea
6. _____ nothing but
7. _____ noticed
8. _____ several
9. _____ elderly
10. _____ skyscraper

a. street level
b. saw
c. went into
d. some
e. before time
f. with great interest
g. not anything
h. surprised
i. didn't know
j. very tall building
k. only
l. old

Definitions

Use your dictionary to define the underlined words as they are used in the sentences.

1. In the United States, there are many farms in the country, but few in the city or suburbs.

   definition _____

   part of speech _____

2. It is very difficult to move from one country to another.

   definition _____

   part of speech _____

3. Karen felt very <u>plain</u> standing next to the beautiful girl.

   definition _____

   part of speech _____

4. Some people like chocolate syrup on their ice cream, but I like to eat mine <u>plain</u>.

   definition _____

   part of speech _____

5. Some people live in the mountains; others live on the <u>plains</u>.

   definition _____

   part of speech _____

6. Put your toys back in the <u>box</u>.

   definition _____

   part of speech _____

7. Some children learn to <u>box</u> to protect themselves.

   definition _____

   part of speech _____

8. Helen waited for the door to <u>close</u>.

   definition _____

   part of speech _____

9. The car was so <u>close</u> Mike was afraid it would hit him.

   definition _____

   part of speech _____

10. It is so <u>close</u> in here, I need to open a window.

    definition _____

    part of speech _____

Sentence Combining

Combine sentences using relative clauses or present participles. Put your relative clause after the underlined word.

> **Example:** The <u>man</u> was walking down the street. He saw a fire.
> a. (relative pronoun) The man who was walking down the street saw a fire.
> b. (present participle) <u>The man walking down the street saw a fire.</u>

1. A country *woman* was visiting the city for the first time. She walked into a very tall building.

   a. (relative clause) _____ -

   _____

   b. (present participle) _____

   _____

2. The old *lady* was standing in front of the door. She went inside.

   a. (relative pronoun) _____

   _____

   b. (present participle) _____

   _____

Topics For Discussion/Writing

○ What misunderstanding occurred in this story? Can you think of another possible ending?

○ Tell a story about a city person in the country or a country person in the city.

○ If there really were a magic box that could make you more attractive, would you go in it? Why or why not?

JUAN BOBO AND THE POT

Before you start to read

- ○ In English Juan Bobo's last name means "silly" or "foolish." There are many stories about Juan Bobo. In each story he misunderstands some information or instruction. As you read this story, think about what Juan Bobo misunderstood this time.

- ○ "Juan" is a Spanish name similar to the English name "John." It is pronounced *Wan*.

- ○ Look at the picture on page 102. Do you think this story takes place in the city or the country? Why?

- ○ In the picture where is Juan Bobo sitting? Does he look happy or angry?

- ○ Stop after paragraph 3. What do you think will happen next?

Juan Bobo and the Pot

JUAN BOBO AND THE POT

1   One day Juan Bobo's mother needed a very big pot. She wanted to make chicken and rice for many people. She said to Juan Bobo, "Go to my friend's house and ask for a big pot. Then come home quickly."

2   Juan Bobo went to the friend's house. She gave him a big pot. He started to carry the pot home. Then he put it down on the road and looked at it. It was very big and heavy. It was made of clay and it had three legs.

3   Then he said to the pot, "You have three legs and I have only two legs. You can carry me for a few minutes." Then Juan Bobo sat down inside the pot. But the pot did not move.

4   Juan Bobo got angry. He threw a stone at the clay pot, and it broke. Then he carried the pieces of the broken pot home.

5   His mother was angry when she saw the broken pot. "You are stupid," she said. But Juan Bobo thought, "I am not a stupid person. Only a fool carries something with three legs."

Exercises

Word Forms

Fill in the blanks with one of the related word forms.

carried	carries	carrying	carry

1. Juan didn't want to _____ the pot.

2. After _____ the pot for awhile, he put it down.

3. He _____ the broken pieces to his mother.

4. Only a stupid person _____ something with three legs.

break	breaking	breaks	broke	broken

1. Be careful not to _____ the pot.

2. He picked up the _____ pieces.

3. This trouble is _____ her heart.

4. Glass _____ easily, so be careful with it.

5. Who _____ the dish that was on the table?

Comprehension

1. What did Juan Bobo's mother want to cook?
2. Why did Juan Bobo's mother need such a big pot?
3. What was the pot made of?
4. Why did Juan Bobo think the pot should carry him?
5. What happened to the pot?
6. How did Juan Bobo's mother feel when he came home?

Sentence Order

Put these sentences in the correct order.

1. _____ Juan Bobo's mother was very angry.

2. _____ The friend gave Juan a big pot.

3. _____ Juan's mother asked him to get a pot from a friend.

4. _____ Juan sat in the pot.

5. _____ Juan started to carry the pot.

6. _____ He threw a stone at the pot.

True–False

1. _____ Juan's mother used the big pot to make dinner.

2. _____ Juan's mother thought Juan was stupid.

3. _____ The friend gave Juan a wood pot.

4. _____ The pot carried Juan home.

5. _____ The pot had three legs.

Reading from Context

Look at paragraph 4 to guess the meaning of the underlined words.

> Juan Bobo got <u>mad</u>. He <u>hurled</u> a <u>rock</u> at the clay pot and <u>smashed</u> it.

What word in paragraph 5 means "stupid person"?

Sentence Combining

Sentences can be combined by reducing one sentence to an adjective. Combine the following sentences. The first one is done for you.

1 a. It was very big and heavy. It was made of clay.

   b. It was a big, heavy, clay pot.

2 a. He was a tall, strong boy. He was French.

   b. _____

3 a. There was an English book on the table. It's small and red.

   b. _____

JUAN BOBO AND THE POT

1   One day Juan Bobo's mother wanted a very large pot. She needed it to make chicken and rice because she was expecting many guests for dinner. She asked Juan Bobo to hurry to a friend's house to borrow a big pot.

2   The friend lent him a large clay pot with three legs. Juan Bobo started to carry it home, but it was very big and heavy. Soon he put the pot down on the road and said to it, "Why don't you carry me for a while, since you have three legs and I only have two?" Of course the pot said nothing. Then Juan Bobo climbed into the pot, but it didn't move.

3   Finally Juan Bobo got mad. He threw a rock at the pot and smashed it. Then he carried the broken pieces home. When his mother saw the broken pieces of the pot, she got angry and told him he was stupid.

4   Juan Bobo wondered why his mother thought he was stupid. He thought to himself, "I'm not stupid. A real fool is one who will carry something that has three legs."

Exercises

Matching

Match the words in the first column with their definitions in the second column.

1. _____ carry
2. _____ fool
3. _____ expecting
4. _____ clay
5. _____ hurry
6. _____ large
7. _____ guest
8. _____ pot
9. _____ smashed
10. _____ pieces
11. _____ wonder

a. broke into pieces
b. small parts, bits
c. a stupid person
d. an invited person
e. a round, deep pan
f. big
g. planning to have
h. to hold while moving
i. to trick
j. want to know
k. go quickly
l. put down
m. heavy earth that can be baked to make dishes

Pronoun References

What word or phrase does each underlined word refer to?

1. "She asked Juan Bobo to hurry to a friend's house.

   she: _____

2. It was very big and heavy.

   it: _____

3. I only have <u>two</u>.

   two: _____

4. <u>He</u> threw a rock at the pot and smashed <u>it</u>.

   he: _____   it: _____

Tense Review

Some of these verbs are regular, and some are irregular. Write the past tense form for each verb. You may use the dictionary if necessary. The first one is done for you.

Present	Past
want	_____
need	_____
is	_____
ask	_____
borrow	_____
lend	_____
carry	_____
throw	_____
get	_____
see	_____
break	_____
tell	_____
think	_____
put	_____
wonder	_____

Synonyms and Antonyms for Vocabulary Development

One word or phrase in each group means the *opposite* of the others. Circle the word that is different.

1. large   big   huge   small   gigantic

2. hurry   rush   go slowly   go quickly

3. smash   fix   break   shatter

4. hold   throw   toss   hurl

5. angry   mad   irate   annoyed   happy

6. stupid   foolish   dumb   smart   idiotic

Dictionary Skills

For each underlined word, write the definition that shows how the word was used in the sentence.

1. Mike <u>wondered</u> if he passed the test.

   definition _____

2. Niagara Falls is one of the natural <u>wonders</u> of the world.

   definition _____

3. The pot had three <u>legs</u>.

   definition _____

4. This <u>leg</u> of my trip takes me to Europe.

   definition _____

5. Mark threw a <u>rock</u> and broke my window.

   definition _____

6. The boat <u>rocked</u> dangerously in the high waves.

   definition _____

7. I like <u>rock</u> music if it isn't too loud.

   definition _____

8. Juan's mother was <u>expecting</u> guests for dinner.

   definition _____

9. Karen must eat properly and rest because she is <u>expecting</u>.

   definition _____

Matching Antonyms

Match the word in the first column with the word in the second column that means its opposite.

1. _____ borrow   a. take
2. _____ broke   b. smart
3. _____ friend   c. lend
4. _____ heavy   d. light
5. _____ nothing   e. slowly
6. _____ quickly   f. fixed
7. _____ stupid   g. something
                           h. enemy
                           i. dumb
                           j. neighbor
                           k. fat

Sentence Combining

Take the groups of sentences in each set and make them into one sentence. You may add some words or leave out some words, but do not change the meaning of the sentences.

1. The friend lent him a pot. It was large. It was made of clay. It had three legs.

   _____

   _____

2. Juan Bobo climbed into the pot. It didn't move.

   _____

   _____

3. Finally Juan Bobo got mad. He threw a rock at the pot. He smashed the pot.

   _____

   _____

4. His mother saw the broken pieces of the pot. She was angry. She told him that he was stupid.

   _____

   _____

Vocabulary from Context

1. What word in paragraph 2 means the opposite of *borrowed*?

   _____

2. What word in paragraph 3 is a synonym for *mad*?

   _____

3. What word in paragraph 1 is a synonym for *big*?

   _____

4. What word in paragraph 4 is a synonym for *stupid*?

   _____

Indirect Speech–Review

The first example is done for you. If you forget how to do this, review the notes in "A Lesson in Persistence."

1 a. She said to Juan, "Go to my friend's house."

  b. <u>She told Juan to go to her friend's house.</u>

2 a. His mother said, "You are stupid."

  b. _____

3 a. The friend said, "Be careful with my pot."

  b. _____

Topics for Discussion/Writing

○ Do you know a real person like Juan Bobo? Tell something funny or silly that person did.

○ Tell a story about a character from a book who always does foolish things.

○ Discuss a foolish thing that you once did that made your parents angry.

THE WOLF AND THE STORK

Before you start to read

○ Look at the pictures. Which animal is the wolf? Which animal is the stork? Describe the wolf. Describe the stork.

○ In the first picture on page 116, what problem does the stork have?

○ In the second picture on page 116, what problem does the wolf have?

○ There is a saying: "He who laughs last, laughs best." What do you think it means? As you read the story, decide how that saying fits the story. Which animal laughs last?

○ This is a story about two old friends. Do you think it teaches a lesson? If so, what is the lesson?

○ Look at the pictures on page 116. Make up a story that explains the pictures. Read the story to see if your idea is similar to the one in the book.

○ Stop after paragraph 3. Guess what the stork will do. Finish reading the story to see if you are right.

1.

2.

The Wolf and the Stork

THE WOLF AND THE STORK

1   A long, long time ago, the wolf and the stork were friends. One day the wolf asked the stork to come to his house to eat.

2   When the stork arrived at the wolf's house, the wolf put two bowls of soup on the table. The wolf ate his bowl of soup quickly. When he finished, he asked the stork, "Did you like my soup?"

3   But the stork was angry because he couldn't eat the soup. His beak was too long! When the stork went home, he was still hungry. The wolf laughed and laughed.

4   Then the stork had an idea. He asked the wolf to come to dinner. He filled two tall pitchers with good food. They began to eat. When the stork finished eating, he asked the wolf if he wanted more to eat.

5   But the wolf was angry. His mouth was so big that he couldn't get it into the pitcher. The wolf went home hungry, and the stork laughed and laughed.

Exercises

Comprehension

1. What food did the wolf serve?
2. Why couldn't the stork eat at the wolf's house?
3. Why couldn't the wolf eat at the stork's house?
4. Do you think the wolf and the stork are still friends? Why or why not?

Matching

Match the words in the first column with their definitions in the second column.

1. _____ fill
2. _____ pitcher
3. _____ bowl
4. _____ idea

5. _____ beak
6. _____ stork
7. _____ angry

a. thought
b. happy
c. a rounded dish
d. the mouth of a bird
e. long-legged bird
f. a dog
g. a tall container for liquids
h. load completely, make full
i. to shop
j. unhappy, upset

True–False

1. _____ The stork couldn't eat from a pitcher.
2. _____ The stork had trouble eating soup from a bowl.
3. _____ The wolf was sorry that his friend couldn't eat the soup.
4. _____ The wolf ate a good meal at the stork's house.
5. _____ The wolf finished his soup quickly.
6. _____ The stork didn't like the soup.

Cloze Exercise

A long, long time ago, the _____ and the stork were friends. One day the wolf asked the _____ to come to his house to eat.

When the stork _____ at the wolf's _____ the wolf put two _____ of soup on the table. He ate his soup _____. When he finished, he _____ the stork, "Did you like my _____?"

But the stork was _____ because he couldn't eat the soup. His _____ was too long! When the stork went home, he was still _____. The wolf laughed and _____.

The stork had an _____. He asked the _____ to come to his house for dinner. He filled two tall _____ with good food. They began to eat. When the stork finished _____, he asked the _____ if he wanted more to eat. But the wolf was angry. His _____ was so big that he couldn't get it into the pitcher. The _____went home hungry, and the _____ laughed and laughed.

New Vocabulary from Context

Look at the story to guess the meaning of the underlined words.

1. (paragraph 1) The wolf invited the stork to come to his house
   to dine.

   invited _____

   dine _____

2. (paragraph 3) But the stork was furious because he couldn't
   eat the soup.

   furious _____

3. (paragraph 4) He filled two pitchers with delicious food.

   delicious _____

4. (paragraph 5) His snout was so big that he couldn't get it into
   the pitcher.

   snout _____

THE WOLF AND THE STORK

1   Long ago a stork and a wolf lived in the countryside. One day the wolf invited his friend the stork to dine at his house. The stork happily agreed to come.

2   When they sat down to eat, the wolf put two bowls of soup on the table. The soup smelled delicious! When the wolf finished eating his soup, he asked the stork how his tasted.

3   But the stork was angry because he couldn't eat the soup with his long beak. When the stork went home hungry, the wolf laughed and laughed.

4   Then the stork decided to get even with the wolf. He invited the wolf to his home for dinner. When the wolf came, the stork filled two pitchers with delicious food. They began to eat. As soon as the stork finished eating, he offered the wolf a second helping.

5   But the wolf was angry because his big snout wouldn't fit in the pitcher. The wolf went home with an empty stomach, and the stork just laughed and laughed.

    Moral: He who laughs last, laughs best.

Exercises

Dictionary Skills

Define the underlined word in each sentence.

1. Stacy filled the <u>pitcher</u> with iced tea.

   definition _____

   part of speech _____

2. Malka was the <u>pitcher</u> on her softball team.

   definition _____

   part of speech _____

3. Robert likes to <u>bowl</u> with his friends.

   definition _____

   part of speech _____

4. Jodie filled the dog's <u>bowl</u> with water.

   definition _____

   part of speech _____

5. Lola exercises regularly because she wants to stay physically <u>fit</u>.

   definition _____

   part of speech _____

6. The stork's beak <u>fit</u> in the pitcher.

   definition _____

   part of speech _____

7. John's father had a <u>fit</u> when John came home at 2:00 A.M.

   definition _____

   part of speech _____

8. Julie has good <u>taste</u>; her clothes always look nice.

   definition _____

   part of speech _____

9. This cake <u>tastes</u> delicious.

   definition _____

   part of speech _____

10. I'd like a second <u>helping</u> of meat.

    definition _____

    part of speech _____

11. Mary is <u>helping</u> her mother in the garden.

    definition _____

    part of speech _____

Idioms

1. *get even* means
   a. have more than
   b. get something new
   c. get back at
   d. be angry at

2. *second helping* means
   a. more help or assistance
   b. more food
   c. two friends
   d. being hungry

3. *have an empty stomach* means
   a. be hungry
   b. be full
   c. be angry
   d. have pains in your stomach

Matching

Match the words in the first column with their definitions in the
second column.

1. _____ dine	a. bad
2. _____ countryside	b. eat supper
3. _____ snout	c. a meal
4. _____ delicious	d. area far from cities and towns
5. _____ taste	e. nose/mouth of some animals
	f. good, tasty
	g. have flavor

Sentence Combining

Use the words in parentheses to combine each pair of sentences.

1. a. The wolf finished his soup. He asked the stork how it tasted.
   b. (When) _____

2. a. The stork was angry. He couldn't eat the soup with his long beak.
   b. (because) _____

3. a. The stork had finished. He offered the wolf a second helping.
   b. (As soon as) _____

Infinitives and Gerunds

finish + ing

Verbs coming after *finish* take the gerund *-ing* form

> **Example:** finish eating—finish shopping

start can be followed by the gerund (*-ing*) or infinitive (*to*) without any difference in meaning.

> **Example:** start dancing or start to dance

stop followed by a gerund (*ing* word) means *don't do that*

> **Example:** Stop talking to your friend. (Don't talk to your friend.)

stop followed by *to* plus verb means *in order to do that* action.

> **Example:** Stop to talk to your friend. (Stop whatever else you are doing in order to talk to your friend.)

In the following sentences, put in the infinitive (*to*) or gerund (*-ing*) form of the word in parentheses.

(eat) 1. The wolf finished _____ the soup.

(laugh) 2. The stork started _____ because the wolf couldn't eat the food.

(study) 3. The students stopped _____ and watched TV instead.

(watch) 4. The students began walking home, but they stopped _____ a basketball game.

(dine) 5. They usually finish _____ at 7:00.

(pop) 6. Children, please stop _____ the balloons; I need them for the party.

Analogies

Analogies are comparisons. In an analogy, you find the relationship between the first two things mentioned, then try to find a word that has the same relationship with the third thing mentioned.

> **Example:** *Young* is to *old* as *little* is to
> a. *big.*   b. *small.*   c. *old.*

The answer is *a. big* because *young* is the opposite of *old* and *little* is the opposite of *big*.

1. *Snout* is to *wolf* as *beak* is to
   a. *mouth.*   b. *animal.*   c. *stork.*   d. *nose.*

2. *Delicious* is to *good* as *terrible* is to
   a. *good.*   b. *bad.*   c. *tasty.*   d. *angry.*

3. *Furious* is to *happy* as *angry* is to
   a. *glad.*   b. *mad.*   c. *sad.*   d. *bad.*

Topics for Discussion/Writing

- Discuss the following expressions and explain how they fit this story.
   a. "He who laughs last, laughs best." Who had the last laugh in this story?
   b. "Don't get mad. Get even." Who got even?
   c. "Revenge is sweet." What is revenge? Who got revenge in this story?
- What do you know about the wolf and stork? Would you like them as friends? Why or why not?
- Did you ever play a trick on a friend, or did anyone ever play a trick on you? How did you feel about it? Explain what happened.

THE TORTOISE AND THE HARE

Before you start to read

○ Look at the picture on page 128. Which animal is the tortoise? What do you know about tortoises?

○ Which animal is the hare? Do you know another name for hare? What do you know about hares?

○ This story is told in different ways in different countries. As you read it, see if you remember a similar story in your own language.

○ Are you more like a tortoise or a hare? In what ways?

The Tortoise and the Hare

1   A long, long time ago, a rabbit and a turtle wanted to have a race. The rabbit was very fast. The turtle was very slow.

2   The night before the race, the turtle went to sleep early. On the morning of the race, he got up early. He started running at 8:00.

3   The rabbit didn't worry about the race. He knew that he was faster than the turtle. The night before the race, he stayed up late at a party. He woke up late for the race. The race started at 8:00, but he didn't start running until 9:00.

4   Because the rabbit was so fast, he quickly passed the turtle. When he was far ahead, he stopped to talk to some friends. He was very busy talking. He didn't see the turtle run past him.

5   The turtle ran and ran. But the rabbit raced past him again. Soon the rabbit was far ahead of the turtle. He thought that he had a lot of time, so he stopped to eat a big lunch. After the rabbit ate, he had to run slowly. He felt very tired from all the food, so he stopped to rest. Soon he fell asleep. While he was sleeping, the turtle passed him again.

6   When the rabbit woke up, he ran very fast. But it was too late. The turtle had won the race.

Exercises

Comprehension

1. Which animal was faster?
2. Which animal prepared for the race? How?
3. What time did the race begin?
4. Why was the rabbit late for the start of the race?
5. Which animal won the race?
6. Tell three things that the rabbit did that caused him to lose the race.

Homonyms

Homonyms are words that sound alike. Choose from the following pairs of words to fill in the blanks.

passed, past   **hare, hair**   **won, one**   **knew, new**

1. The rabbit _____ that he was faster than the turtle.
2. The rabbit quickly _____ the turtle.
3. Lisa has beautiful brown _____.
4. Another word for rabbit is _____.
5. While the hare was sleeping, the turtle ran _____ him.
6. Because he never stopped running, the turtle _____ the race.
7. I just bought a _____ car.
8. I like your car so much that I may buy _____ just like it.

Sentence Combining

Use the word in parentheses to combine the two sentences.

1. The rabbit had a lot of time. He stopped to eat a big lunch.

   (so) _____

2. The rabbit was very fast. The turtle was very slow.

   (but) _____

3. The rabbit ate. He had to run slowly.

   (After) _____

4. He felt tired from all the food. He had to rest.

   (so . . . that) _____

5. He was sleeping. The turtle passed him again.

   (While) _____

True–False

1. _____ The rabbit was faster than the turtle.
2. _____ The rabbit didn't start the race on time.
3. _____ The turtle stopped to have lunch.
4. _____ The rabbit stopped to talk to some friends.
5. _____ The rabbit was faster so he won the race.
6. _____ The rabbit couldn't run fast after he ate.
7. _____ The rabbit slept soon after he ate.
8. _____ The rabbit went to a party the night before the race.
9. _____ The turtle went to sleep late the night before the race.
10. _____ The rabbit started running at 8:00.

Sentence Order

Put these sentences in the correct order.

1. _____ The rabbit woke up in the morning.
2. _____ The turtle started running in the race.
3. _____ The rabbit ate a big lunch.
4. _____ The rabbit started running in the race.
5. _____ The rabbit went to a party.
6. _____ The turtle won the race.
7. _____ The rabbit stopped to talk to his friends.
8. _____ The rabbit fell asleep.
9. _____ The rabbit and the turtle wanted to have a race.
10. _____ The turtle passed the rabbit for the last time.

Reading From Context

Look at the words in the story to guess the meaning of the underlined words.

1. Because the hare was so quick, he soon overtook the tortoise. (paragraph 4)

   hare _____   quick _____

   overtook _____   tortoise _____

2. When the hare was far out in front he paused to chat with some buddies. (paragraph 4)

   out in front _____   paused _____

   chat _____   buddies _____

3. He felt exhausted from all the food, so he stopped to take a nap. (paragraph 5)

   exhausted _____   take a nap _____

The Tortoise
and the Hare

1   Once upon a time, a tortoise and a hare decided to have a race. The hare was a very fast runner, but the tortoise was very slow.

2   To prepare for the race, the tortoise went to sleep early. On the morning of the race, he woke up promptly so he could be at the starting line at 8:00.

3   The hare didn't prepare for the race because he knew that he was faster than the tortoise. The hare stayed up late at a party. On the morning of the race, he overslept. Although he was supposed to start running at 8:00, he didn't begin until 9:00.

4   Because the hare was so quick, he soon overtook the tortoise. When the hare was out in front, he paused to chat with some friends. The hare was so busy talking that he didn't see the tortoise pass him.

5   The tortoise went steadily on and on. He never stopped or rested. But the hare raced past him again and was soon very far ahead. The hare was hungry, so he stopped to have a big meal. When he was full, he couldn't run very fast. All the food made him feel so sleepy that he stopped to take a nap.

6   While the hare was sleeping, the tortoise passed him again. When the hare awoke, he raced as fast as he could. But he was too late! The tortoise had already crossed the finish line.

Exercises

Character Description

Look at the following words. Write the words that describe the rabbit in the rabbit column. Write the ones that describe the turtle in the turtle column. You may use a dictionary to help you with the words.

prompt   slow   consistent   late
irresponsible   steady   over-confident
reliable   persistent   fast

rabbit   **turtle**

1.   1.

2.   2.

3.   3.

4.   4.

                              5.

                              6.

Synonyms and Antonyms

One word or phrase in each group doesn't belong. Circle the word or phrase that does not mean the same as the others.

1. swift   slow   fast   quick

2. prompt   on time   late   timely

3. overtake   pass   run past   fall behind

4. wake up   take a nap   rest   sleep

5. out in front   in the rear   ahead   in the lead

Comprehension

1. Why didn't the rabbit go to sleep early the night before the race?
2. Why did the rabbit take a nap?
3. The hare was much faster than the tortoise, but the tortoise was ahead at the beginning, the middle, and the end of the race. How did the tortoise get ahead each time?
4. What time was the race supposed to start?
5. What time did the hare start running?

Synonyms

Match the words in the first column with the definition in the second column.

1. _____ ahead
2. _____ chat
3. _____ cross the finish line
4. _____ hare
5. _____ meal
6. _____ overslept
7. _____ overtook
8. _____ paused

9. _____ prepare
10. _____ promptly
11. _____ quick

12. _____ steadily
13. _____ starting line
14. _____ take a nap
15. _____ tortoise
16. _____ supposed to

a. complete the race
b. food eaten at one time
c. fast
d. get ready
e. in front
f. on time
g. passed in front of
h. place where a race begins
i. a kind of rabbit
j. sleep for a short time
k. stopped for a short time
l. have a conversation
m. a kind of turtle
n. at an even speed
o. woke up late
p. expected to

Gerunds and Infinitives

Write the word in parentheses in the gerund (*ing*) form or infinitive (*to*) form.

1. The tortoise never stopped (run) _____, but the hare stopped (chat) _____ with his friends.

2. (Prepare) _____ for the race, the tortoise went (sleep) _____ early.

3. The tortoise was hungry, so he stopped (have) _____ a big meal.

4. The food made him sleepy, so he stopped (take) _____ a nap.

5. The tortoise never stopped (rest) _____.

6. The tortoise started (run) _____ at 8:00.

Topics for Discussion/Writing

○ How is the tortoise in this story like the ants in "The Ant and the Cicada?" How is the hare similar to the cicadas?

○ There is a saying: "Slow but steady wins the race." How does that saying describe what happened in this story?

○ In a poem called "Don't Quit," one line says "The race is not always to the swift." In this story, who was swift? Who didn't quit?

○ Are you more like the tortoise or the hare? In what way?

○ Do you know a person like the tortoise? Do you know a person like the hare? Which one would you rather work with? Why?

THE SHADOW

Before you start to read

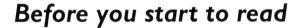

○ This is a story of a mistake that caused great sorrow (sadness) for a whole family. Do you think this story has a lesson? If so, what do you think that lesson is?

○ Have you ever jumped to a conclusion (made your opinion about someone or something *before* you had all of the facts) and then found out you were wrong?

○ Stop after paragraph 2. What do you think will happen when the real father comes home?

○ Have you ever heard of the story *Othello*? Discuss it briefly before you read this story.

1.

2.

3.

4.

5.

THE SHADOW

1   A long time ago during wartime, a soldier went away to fight. His wife was expecting a baby. The baby was born soon after he left.

2   When the baby learned to talk, he always asked his mother, "Where is my father?" The mother got tired of his questions. One night she pointed to her shadow on the wall and said, "This is your father." After that she pointed to her shadow every night at dinner and said that his father would eat dinner with them. This made the little boy feel happy.

3   Finally the war was over. The husband came home. But when he arrived at his house, the wife was out. He saw the little boy. He knew it was his son, but the little boy said, "You are not my father. He won't be home until dinner time."

4   The father was very angry. Then his wife arrived. He said that she had been a bad wife, and he would not listen to her. Then the wife felt so sad that she jumped into the river and killed herself.

5   That night the boy saw his father's shadow on the wall. He pointed to it and said, "Now my father is home." Then the man understood. But it was too late!

Exercises

True–False

1. _____ The wife was a bad wife.
2. _____ The boy did not know his father when he saw him.
3. _____ The boy was only a little baby when his father went to fight.
4. _____ The mother killed herself.
5. _____ The boy's father came home at dinner time.

Vocabulary from Context

Look at the words in the original story to guess the meaning of the underlined words.

1. "His wife was <u>pregnant</u>."(paragraph 1)

   pregnant _____

2. "He <u>accused</u> her of being <u>unfaithful</u>, and he <u>refused</u> to listen to her." (paragraph 4)

   accused _____

   unfaithful _____

   refuse _____

3. "Then the man <u>realized</u> what had happened." (paragraph 5)

   realized _____

Matching

Match the words in the first column with their definitions in the second column.

1. _____ expecting
2. _____ pointed
3. _____ shadow
4. _____ finally
5. _____ arrived
6. _____ soldier

a. wanting
b. a person in an army
c. showed with a finger
d. waiting for, waiting to have
e. a dark area caused by something blocking the light
f. soon
g. came
h. went away
i. at last

Sentence Order

Put these sentences in the correct order.

1. _____ The father left to fight in the war.
2. _____ The child asked, "Where is my father?"
3. _____ The wife had a baby.
4. _____ The father understood that his wife was a good wife.
5. _____ The wife killed herself.
6. _____ The woman told her son that her shadow was his father.

Comprehension

1. The last sentence says, "But it was too late!" Why was it too late?
2. Why did the woman tell her son that the shadow was his father?
3. Why didn't the boy know his father?
4. Why was the father angry at his wife?
5. How did the wife kill herself?
6. When did the father understand that his wife had been a good wife?

Sentence Combining

Use the word in parentheses to combine the sentences.

1. a. The baby learned to talk. He always asked his mother questions.

   b. (when) _____

2. a. The wife felt sad. She jumped into the river and killed herself. (so . . . that) _____

3. a. The soldier went away to fight. His wife had a baby.

   b. (after) _____

THE SHADOW

1   A long time ago during wartime, a soldier went away to fight. His wife was pregnant when he left.

2   When the baby was old enough, he became unhappy because he saw that other children had fathers. He kept asking his mother where his father was.

3   One night when she got tired of his questions, the mother pointed to her shadow on the wall. She told the boy that the shadow was his father. From that day on, she pointed to her shadow every night at dinner time and said that his father would eat dinner with them. Then the boy was happy because he thought that his father was with him.

4   Finally, when the war ended, the husband came home. But his wife was out, and only the little boy was home. The soldier knew that the boy was his son, but the boy said, "You are not my father. He won't be home until dinner time."

5   The father was very upset. When his wife came home, he accused her of being unfaithful, and he refused to listen to her. She felt so sad that she went to the river and drowned herself.

6   That evening, the boy saw his father's shadow on the wall. He pointed to it and said, "Now my father is home." Then the man realized what had happened. But it was too late!

Exercises

Dictionary Skills

Use your dictionary. Write the definition of the underlined word that fits how the word was used in the sentence.

1. The mother <u>pointed</u> to her shadow.

   definition _____

   part of speech _____

2. What is the <u>point</u> of this story?

   definition _____

   part of speech _____

3. I broke the <u>point</u> on my pencil.

   definition _____

   part of speech _____

4. The father was very <u>upset</u>.

   definition _____

   part of speech _____

5. The child <u>upset</u> his glass of milk.

   definition _____

   part of speech _____

Matching

Match the words in the first column with their definitions in the second column.

1. _____ upset
2. _____ accuse

3. _____ refused
4. _____ pregnant
5. _____ from that day on
6. _____ evening
7. _____ realized

8. _____ unfaithful

a. expecting a baby
b. blame; say someone did something wrong

c. would not
d. promised
e. before
f. early night
g. came to understand

h. truly
i. after that day
j. disloyal; untrue
k. angry or unhappy about something

Synonyms and Antonyms

Circle the word or phrase in each group that is different than the others. You may use your dictionary.

1. sadness	sorrow	grief	joy
2. mistrust	trust	jealousy	suspicion
3. accuse	blame	thank	say someone is guilty
4. point	indicate	show with a finger	ask

Reading from Context

Look at the fourth paragraph in story A to find out the meaning of the underlined words from story B.

> The father was very underlined{upset}. When the wife arrived, he accused her of being unfaithful, and he refused to listen to her.

Comprehension

1. "Then the man realized what had happened." What had happened?
2. Why did the woman kill herself?
3. Why did the father leave his wife?
4. Why didn't the boy know his father?
5. *He* pointed to *it*. (paragraph 5)

   a. Who was he?   b. What was it?

Prefix Review

Find two words in this story that use the prefix *un-* meaning *not*.

1. _____   2. _____

Perspective

Tell this story from the point of view of the father. Paragraph 1 is done for you. Do paragraphs 4, 5, 6.

> A long time ago, during wartime, I went away to fight. My wife was pregnant when I left.

Tell this story from the point of view of the wife. Do paragraphs 2–5.

> A long time ago during wartime, my husband, a soldier, went away to fight. I was pregnant when he left.

Topics for Discussion/Writing

○ In the pre-reading exercise, you heard the story of Othello. How is that story similar to this one? How is it different?

○ Do you think this story teaches a lesson? What is the lesson.

○ Tell about an incident when someone jumped to a conclusion (reached a decision before they knew all the facts) and then found out that he/she was wrong. Tell what happened.

DON'T MAKE A BARGAIN WITH A FOX

Before you start to read

○ Animals are given different traits in different cultures.

For example, we say: "As busy as a bee." "As stubborn as a mule." "As strong as an ox." "As fast as a rabbit (hare)." "As sly (smart and tricky) as a fox." Read this story and explain how this fox was sly.

○ Can you think of other sayings that use animals to describe human qualities?

○ The title says, "Don't make a bargain with a fox." What is a bargain? Why shouldn't you make a bargain with a fox?

1.

2.

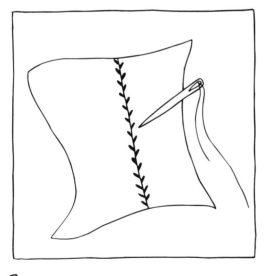

3.

4.

Don't Make a Bargain with a Fox

Don't Make a Bargain with a Fox

1   It was very cold. Two rabbits were playing in a field. Far away they saw two small red things. The rabbits went closer to look.

2   The two red things were pieces of an old red blanket. The pieces were warm and thick, but they were very small. They were too small to use.

3   Soon a fox came by. "Good day, my friends," he said. "You look worried. Do you have a problem?" The rabbits answered, "Yes! We need a needle and thread to sew the pieces of the blanket together." "You can use my needle and thread if I can use the blanket, too," said the fox.

4   The rabbits used the fox's needle and thread. When the rabbits finished their sewing, the fox looked at their work. "You did a good job," he said. "I'll see you tonight."

5   Night came, and the wind was very cold. The fox came back to the rabbits. "Good evening, my friends. It's a cold, cold night. But we will be warm! We have the nice, warm blanket you sewed with my needle and

thread. You sewed down the middle of the blanket. The right thing is for me to sleep in the middle." "Yes, that's right Mr. Fox," said the rabbits.

6   So the fox lay down on the ground. The rabbits put the middle of the blanket over him. The blanket covered him, but it did not cover the rabbits. They were cold all night!

7   So you see, you should never make a bargain with a fox. He will always win.

Exercises

Vocabulary

Choose from the following words to fill in the blanks:

bargain	blanket	closer	field	friends	thick
middle	worried	piece	thread	problem	

1. At night, the mother kissed her child and covered him with a

    _____.

2. When you sew this coat, make sure the _____

    is the same color as the material.

3. Because the blanket is _____, it is

    very warm.

4. As the big dog got _____, the little dog

    ran away.

5. Only make a _____ with someone you

    can trust.

6. Please put the dish on the _____ shelf.

7. Ahmed and Jerry went to the _____ to

    play ball.

8. You should ask for help when you have a _____.

True–False

1. _____ The fox was warm all night.
2. _____ The rabbits found two big pieces of a blanket.
3. _____ The fox thought that he should sleep in the middle because he sewed the blanket up the middle.
4. _____ The rabbits sewed the blanket together.
5. _____ The blanket kept the rabbits warm all night.

Sentence Order

Put these sentences in the correct order.

1. _____ The rabbits sewed the two pieces of blanket.
2. _____ The rabbits were cold all night.
3. _____ The rabbits saw two red things.
4. _____ The fox lent the rabbits his needle and thread.
5. _____ The fox lay down between the two rabbits.

Animal Sayings

Choose from the following animals to complete these sayings about animals.

bird	dog	pig	owl
fox	turtle	ox	rabbit

1. Fast as a _____.
2. Eat like a _____. (eat very little)
3. Sly as a _____.
4. Work like a _____.
5. Slow as a _____.

6. Eat like a _____.(eat a lot or eat sloppily)

7. Strong as an _____.

8. Wise as an _____.

Homonyms

The following words sound alike but look different. Choose from the following homonyms to fill in the blanks.

piece, peace	**to, two, too**
sew, so	**red, read**

1. Martin Luther King wanted _____ for all people.

2. Anita _____ the book yesterday.

3. _____ is Han's favorite color.

4. This movie is _____ long.

5. The rabbits saw _____ red things.

6. The red thing was a _____ of a blanket.

7. The fox said that he wanted _____ share the blanket.

Comprehension

1. What were the two red things?
2. Who had a needle and thread?
3. Who sewed the blanket?
4. Why did the fox think that he should sleep in the middle?
5. In what season did this story take place? How do you know?

Don't Make a Bargain with a Fox

1   On a very cold winter's day, two rabbits were playing together in the snow. In the distance, they saw two red spots. They went closer to have a look.

2   The two spots were pieces of an old red blanket. The pieces were thick, but very, very small. In fact, they were too small to use.

3   Just then a fox came by. He greeted the rabbits. "You look upset," he said. "What's the problem?" The rabbits explained that they wanted to sew the two pieces of blanket together, but they didn't have a needle and thread. So the fox said that he would lend them his needle and thread if they would share the blanket with him.

4   When the rabbits finished sewing, the fox looked at their work. "Not bad," he said. "See you fellows tonight!"

5   At night it got very cold, and the wind blew hard. Soon the fox returned. He wasn't worried about the cold. "We have the nice blanket that you sewed with the needle and thread I loaned you. You sewed it up the middle, so the middle part should be mine!"

6   Then the fox lay down on the ground. The rabbits put the middle of the blanket over him. Then they lay down on either side of the fox. But there wasn't enough blanket to cover the poor rabbits, so they shivered all night.

7   That's why some people say it's a bad idea to make a bargain with a fox. He will beat you every time!

Exercises

Matching

Match the words in the first column with their definitions in the second column.

1. _____ cover
2. _____ fellows
3. _____ greeted
4. _____ in fact
5. _____ in the distance
6. _____ loaned
7. _____ returned
8. _____ share
9. _____ shivered
10. _____ spot
11. _____ bargain
12. _____ on either side
13. _____ explained

a. place something over something else
b. guys
c. shook from the cold
d. really
e. worried or angry
f. lent
g. came back
h. use together
i. said hello
j. said that
k. a small mark, dot
l. far away
m. on the same side
n. on each side
o. field
p. deal, agreement

Vocabulary Development–Homonyms

Homonyms are words that sound alike. Use the correct words to fill in the blanks.

1. **(sew, so)**

   I want to _____ this, _____ I need a needle and thread.

2. **blew, blue**

   The wind _____ so hard, that I turned _____ from the cold.

3. **(there, their, they're)**

   _____ going to Chicago to visit _____ aunt who lives _____.

4. **(two, to, too)**

   I need _____ buy _____ books and some paper, _____.

5. **(piece, peace)**

   If the children would share this _____ of candy instead of fighting over it, we could have some _____ in this house.

Synonyms

Most of the words or phrases in each group are synonyms. Circle the one word or phrase that does not belong .

1. shiver	stand still	shake	tremble
2. in the distance	afar	far away	nearby
3. in fact	really	maybe	truly
4. fight	bargain	deal	agreement

Vocabulary

Choose from the following words to fill in the blanks:

| bargain | cold | fellows | loaned |
| pieces | sew | shivered | thread |

1. The children _____ because they played too
   long in the cold.

2. Did any of you _____ see my new game?

3. Never make a _____ with a person you
   don't trust.

4. How many _____ of meat do you want?

5. I will _____ the torn coat so I can wear
   it again.

Dictionary Skills

Write the definition for the underlined word that best shows how the
word was used in the sentence.

1. Lois got a <u>spot</u> on her new dress.

   definition _____

   part of speech _____

2. Did you <u>spot</u> the mockingbird that was singing in the tree?

   definition _____

   part of speech _____

3. The rabbits made a bad <u>bargain</u> with the fox.

   definition _____

   part of speech _____

4. Jane bought this dress on sale; it was a real <u>bargain</u>.

   definition _____

   part of speech _____

The following words change pronunciation depending on their usage.

5. Mary and John walked <u>close</u> to the woods.

   definition _____

   part of speech _____

   pronunciation _____

6. Please <u>close</u> the door when you leave.

   definition _____

   part of speech _____

   pronunciation _____

7. The <u>wind</u> blew so the man pulled his coat around him.

   definition _____

   part of speech _____

   pronunciation _____

8. Did Jim <u>wind</u> the clock?

   definition _____

   part of speech _____

   pronunciation _____

Comprehension

1. What season was it? List three phrases from the story that tell you about the weather.
2. What did the rabbits contribute to the blanket? What did the fox contribute?
3. List three things that you learned about the rabbits from reading this story.
4. What do you know about the fox?

Sentence Combining

Use the word in parentheses to combine the sentences.

1 a. The rabbits finished sewing. The fox looked at their work.

  b. (when) _____

2 a. The rabbits explained. They wanted to sew the two pieces together.

  b. (that) _____

3 a. There wasn't enough blanket. The rabbits shivered all night.

  b. (so) _____

Topics for Discussion

○ What bargain did the fox make with the rabbits? Was this bargain fair? Why or why not?
○ Have you ever made a bad bargain? Tell about it.
○ Do you know any other stories that tell about the sly (smart and tricky) character of the fox?

A Thief's Story

Before you start to read

○ What is a thief? Why do people become thieves?

○ What happens to thieves who are caught?

○ How do children learn the difference between right and wrong? Who are a child's first teachers?

1.

2.

3.

A Thief's Story

1   Once upon a time, there was a poor family. They had one son. The son often went out to steal things. Every time he brought something home, his mother was happy. She didn't ask him how and where he got it. She just said, "That's very good."

2   Many years passed. The little boy grew up and became a full-time thief. One day the police caught him and took him to jail. The court said that he must die for his crimes. But before dying, he could have one last wish.

The son asked for his mother. He said that he wanted
3   to see her tongue. The mother came and stuck out her tongue. Then the son cut his mother's tongue until it was bleeding. Everyone was surprised. They wanted to know why he hurt his mother.

4   The son answered, " My mother did not tell me it was wrong to steal. And so I am here now."

5   The court judge decided that the son should not die. The judge let the son go free. The son became an honest man and lived to an old age.

Exercises

Word Forms

Fill in the blanks with the correct form of the the words.

bled   **bleed**   **bleeding**   **bleeds**   **blood**

1. Marty's nose is _____.
2. The patient has lost a lot of _____.
3. When Tim cut his finger, it _____.

steal   **stealing**   **steals**   **stole**   **stolen**

4. The police found the thief in the _____ car.
5. A person who _____ may go to jail.
6. This is the man who _____ your car yesterday.

bring   **bringing**   **brings**   **brought**

7. Mike always _____ us pizza.
8. Long ago the boy _____ his mother some stolen eggs.
9. What are you _____ her for her birthday?

Comprehension

1. What story opener was used?
2. Many American stories end: "He lived happily ever after." What ending is used in this story?
3. Why did the thief cut his mother's tongue?
4. Where did the boy get the things that he brought to his mother?
5. How did his mother act when he stole things for her?
6. What is the subject of the first sentence? What is the verb?
7. What happened to the thief at the end of the story?

True–False

1. _____ The little boy went to jail because he stole eggs for his mother.
2. _____ The son cut his mother's tongue.
3. _____ The mother didn't want her son to steal.
4. _____ The son died because he was a thief.
5. _____ The police took the son to jail.
6. _____ The son was angry at his mother.
7. _____ The mother was a thief.
8. _____ The court judge decided that the son should not die.
9. _____ The thief became an honest man.
10. _____ The thief was young when he died.

Sentence Order

Put these sentences in the correct order.

1. _____ The police caught the son.
2. _____ The mother said, "That's very good."
3. _____ He became an honest man.
4. _____ He cut his mother's tongue.
5. _____ He went to jail.
6. _____ The court said he must die.
7. _____ The boy brought his mother some eggs.
8. _____ He became a full-time thief.
9. _____ His mother stuck out her tongue.
10. _____ He was given one last wish.

Past Tense Review

Put the following irregular verbs in the past tense.

Present tense	Past Tense
1. go	_____
2. stick	_____
3. come	_____
4. tell	_____
5. cut	_____
6. steal	_____
7. become	_____
8. bleed	_____
9. take	_____
10. catch	_____

Sound/Spelling

Some words end in *gue* but the *ue* is silent.
Say these words:

tongue   **dialogue**   **catalogue**

Some words ending in *f* form their plural by changing the *f* to *v* and adding *es*.

Write the plural for the following words. The first one is done for you.

Singular	Plural
1. thief	thieves
2. knife	_____
3. life	_____
4. wife	_____

Vocabulary

Match the word in the first column with its definition in the second column.

1. _____ stick out   a. take something that belongs to someone else

2. _____ steal   b. a person who can make legal decisions in court; to make a legal decision

3. _____ crime   c. unlawful act

4. _____ bleed   d. put out, push out

5. _____ court   e. the place where law decisions are made

6. _____ judge   f. punishment

7. _____ honest   g. lose red fluid in the body

      h. trustworthy, truthful

Sentence Patterns

There is; There are

In sentences beginning with "There is" or "There are," the subject comes after the verb and the verb agrees with that subject.

> **Example:** There was a poor man.
>
> > **Subject:** <u>man</u> **Verb:** <u>was</u>
> >
> > There are many books on the table.

In the following sentences underline the subject and write *is* or *are* in the blank.

1. There _____ a new moon tonight.

2. There _____ also many stars in the sky.

3. There _____ many thieves in jail.

4. There _____ several stories in this book.

5. There _____ a moral to this story.

A Thief's Story

1   Once upon a time, there was a poor family who had one son. He used to go out and steal things. Whatever he brought home, his mother accepted. Once he brought back some eggs. Instead of asking him how and where he got them, she just praised him and said, "Well done!"

2   Years passed. The little boy grew up and became a professional thief. The police arrested him and took him to prison. The court sentenced him to death for his crimes. When he was given one last request, he asked the jailers to bring his mother to him so that he could see her tongue.

3   When the mother came, she stuck her tongue out. The son reached over and cut it until it bled! Everyone was astonished and wondered why he had done such a thing.

4   The son explained: "Instead of warning me not to steal, my mother praised me. If she had told me it was wrong to take things that belong to someone else, I would not be here now."

5   Later the judge gave him a pardon. The son became an honest man and lived to a ripe old age.

171

Exercises

Matching

Match the words in the first column with their definitions in the second column.

1. _____ accepted
2. _____ arrested
3. _____ astonished
4. _____ belong to
5. _____ brought
6. _____ explained
7. _____ pardon
8. _____ honest
9. _____ instead

10. _____ jailers
11. _____ praised
12. _____ professional
13. _____ wrong
14. _____ ripe

15. _____ sentenced
16. _____ stuck out
17. _____ used to
18. _____ warning
19. _____ well done
20. _____ wondered

21. _____ request

a. anything that . . .
b. good work
c. told the reason
d. surprised
e. stopped by police
f. took what was offered
g. pushed out
h. congratulated
i. people who work in prison
j. forgive officially
k. be the property of
l. in place of
m. carried to
n. doing a job to earn money
o. did in the past
p. truthful, trustworthy
q. were curious about
r. bad, improper
s. mature, fully grown
t. gave punishment for breaking the law
u. making aware of harm or danger
v. ask for something

Sentence Combining

Use the words in parentheses to combine each pair of sentences into one sentence.

1 a. There was a poor family. They had one son.

   b. (who) _____

2 a. The mother came. She stuck out her tongue.

   b. (when) _____

3 a. He brought things home. His mother accepted them.

   b. (whenever) _____

Vocabulary Development

All of the following words relate to the legal system. Some were in the story. Others were not. Discuss the meaning of these words.

thief	arrest	police	prison
jailer	court	trial	sentence
last request	pardon	jury	judge

Can you write a short story using at least five of these words?

Synonyms and Antonyms

Circle the word or phrase in each group that doesn't mean the same as the others.

1. request	ask for	give		
2. evil	honest	trustworthy	truthful	
3. instead of	because of	in place of	in lieu of	
4. prison	home	jail	penal institution	
5. thief	crook	burglar	robber	judge

Dictionary Skills

Define the underlined word as it is used in the sentence.

1. Define the underlined word as it is used in this <u>sentence</u>.

    definition _____

    part of speech _____

2. The court <u>sentenced</u> him to five years in jail.

    definition _____

    part of speech _____

3. He cut his mother's <u>tongue</u>.

    definition _____

    part of speech _____

4. What is your native <u>tongue</u>?

    definition _____

    part of speech _____

Topics for Discussion

- ○ If you were the judge in this story, would you have sentenced the thief to death? Why or why not?
- ○ If you were the judge, would you have pardoned the thief? Why or why not?
- ○ Is there a moral to this story? What is it?
- ○ "Everyone wondered why he had done such a thing." (paragraph 5) What did he do? Why did he do it? Was he right or wrong to do it?
- ○ Is it ever right or excusable to steal? Explain your answer.
- ○ Discuss the saying "As the twig is bent, so the tree inclines." What does that saying have to do with this story?
- ○ Discuss the saying "Honesty is the best policy." What does it have to do with this story?

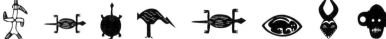

THE STORY OF
THE SMART PARROT

Before you start to read

○ Look at picture #1 on page 176. What kind of animal is
a parrot?

○ Have you ever heard a talking bird? Parrots are talking
birds that can repeat words or sounds that they hear. Do
you think they can understand the words they hear or say?

○ The bird in this story is stubborn (determined to do
something others don't want him to do or not to do
something others want him to do). Have you ever been
stubborn? Have you ever refused to do something that you
were able to do?

○ Read to the end of paragraph 5. What do you think the
man saw?

1.

2.

3.

4.

THE STORY OF THE SMART PARROT

1   A man in Puerto Rico had a wonderful parrot. There was no other parrot like him. He was very, very smart. This parrot could say any word—except one. He would *not* say the name of the town where he was born. The name of that town was Cataño.

2   The man tried and tried to teach the parrot to say "Cataño." But the bird would not say the word. At first the man was very nice, but then he got angry. "You stupid bird! Why can't you say that word? Say Cataño or I'll kill you!" But the parrot would not say it. Then the man got so angry that he shouted over and over, "Say Cataño or I'll kill you." But the bird wouldn't talk.

3   One day after trying for many hours to make the bird say Cataño, the man got very, very angry. He picked up the bird and threw him into the chicken house. "You are more stupid than the chickens. Soon I will eat them, and I will eat you, too."

4   In the chicken house there were four old chickens. They were for Sunday dinner. The man put the parrot in the chicken house and left.

5   The next day the man came back to the chicken house. He opened the door and stopped. He was very surprised at what he saw!

6   He saw three dead chickens on the floor. The parrot was screaming at the fourth chicken, "Say Cataño or I'll kill you!"

Exercises

True–False

1. _____ The parrot could not say "Cataño."
2. _____ The parrot would not say "Cataño" for the man.
3. _____ The chickens couldn't say "Cataño."
4. _____ The parrot was more stupid than the chickens.
5. _____ The man ate the parrot for dinner.
6. _____ The man killed the chickens.
7. _____ The man got angry at the parrot.
8. _____ The parrot could say many words.
9. _____ The parrot killed the chickens.
10. _____ Cataño was the name of the parrot.

Sentence Order

Put the sentences in the correct order.

1. _____ The man saw three dead chickens on the floor.
2. _____ The man tried to teach the parrot to say "Cataño."
3. _____ The man threw the parrot into the chicken house.
4. _____ The parrot yelled, "Say Cataño or I'll kill you."
5. _____ The man said, "Say Cataño or I'll kill you."

Comprehension

1. What word wouldn't the parrot say?
2. What did the man do to the parrot?
3. What did the man want to do with the chickens?
4. Why was the man surprised when he went to the chicken house?
5. How did the three chickens die?
6. Cataño was
    a. the bird's name
    b. the man's name
    c. the name of the town
7. "The parrot would not say *it*" (paragraph 2). What wouldn't the parrot say?
8. Where did this story take place?
9. The parrot could say any word except *one*. What does *one* mean in that sentence?
10. Why was the parrot so wonderful?

Sentence Combining

Use the words in parentheses to combine the sentences. Sometimes you may have to change the sentence slightly when you combine.

1 a. At first the man was very nice. He got angry.

   b. (but then) _____

2 a. He opened the door and stopped. He was very surprised at what he saw.

   b. (because) _____

3 a. He opened the door. He was very surprised at what he saw.

   b. (when) _____

4 a. In the chicken house there were four old chickens. They were for Sunday's dinner.

   b. (that) _____

Synonyms

Three words in each group are similar in meaning. Circle the word that is different.

1. chicken   man   bird   parrot

2. screaming   yelling   shouting   trying

3. angry   wonderful   amazing   surprising

THE STORY OF THE SMART PARROT

1   There was once a man in Puerto Rico who had a wonderful parrot. The parrot was unique; there was no other like him in the whole world. He could learn to say any word—except one. He could not say the name of his native town, Cataño.

2   The man did everything he could to teach the parrot to say "Cataño," but he never succeeded. At first he was very gentle with the bird, but gradually he lost his temper. "You stupid bird! Why can't you learn to say that one word? Say 'Cataño' or I'll kill you!" But the parrot would not say it. Many times the man screamed, "Say Cataño or I'll kill you!" But the bird would not repeat the name.

3   Finally the man gave up. He picked up the parrot and threw him into the chicken house. "You are even more stupid than the chickens," he said

4   In the chicken house there were four old chickens, waiting to be killed for Sunday's dinner.

5   The next morning, the man went out to the chicken house. When he opened the door, he was shocked by what he saw. He could not believe his eyes and ears!

6   On the floor lay three dead chickens. The parrot was screaming at the fourth, "Say Cataño or I'll kill you!"

Exercises

Matching

Match the words in the first column with their definitions in the
second column.

1. _____ except   a. but not
2. _____ finally   b. lifted
3. _____ gave up   c. did what one
                              wanted to do
4. _____ gentle   d. yelled
5. _____ gradually   e. take
6. _____ lost his temper f. one of a kind
7. _____ native   g. lately
8. _____ picked up   h. slowly, over a period
                              of time
9. _____ repeat   i. say something after
                              hearing it
10. _____ screamed   j. very surprised
11. _____ shocked   k. at last
12. _____ succeeded   l. got angry
13. _____ unique   m. considerate, kind
                           n. quit
                           o. original, by birth

Synonyms

Circle the one word in each group that doesn't belong.

1. shocked   happy   amazed   astounded
2. quickly   gradually   slowly   eventually
3. lost his temper got angry   got mad   was shocked

Sentence Combining

1 a. There was once a man in Puerto Rico. He had a wonderful parrot.

  b. (who) _____

2 a. The man opened the door. He was shocked by what he saw.

  b (when) _____

3 a. There were four old chickens. They were waiting to be killed for Sunday's dinner.

  b (reduce the second sentence to a present participle)

  _____

4 a. The man had a parrot. The parrot was unique.

  b. (use only the word *unique* from the second sentence.)

  _____

Definitions from Context

1. What phrase in paragraph 1 tells the meaning of *unique*?

  _____

2. What phrase in paragraph 1 means the place where one is born and raised? _____

3. What phrase in paragraph 2 means slowly got angry?

  _____

4. What phrase in paragraph 5 explains the meaning of *shocked*?

  _____

Dictionary Definitions

Define the underlined word the way it is used in the sentence.

1. The man lost his <u>temper</u>.

   definition _____

   part of speech _____

2. In "A Thief's Story," the judge <u>tempered</u> justice with mercy.

   definition _____

   part of speech _____

3. The pole was made of <u>tempered</u> steel.

   definition _____

   part of speech _____

4. The man was <u>shocked</u> by what he saw.

   definition _____

   part of speech _____

5. The man was <u>shocked</u> when he touched the electric wire.

   definition _____

   part of speech _____

Comprehension

1. "On the floor lay three dead chickens." What is the subject of that sentence? What is the verb? The sentence has an unusual word order. What is a more common way to say the same thing? Why do you think the author used this word order?

2. "He could not believe his eyes" means:
   a. He didn't like his eyes.
   b. He couldn't see.
   c. He saw something unbelievable.
   d. He had unbelievable eyes.

3. What is the subject of the first sentence of the story? What is the verb?

4. How do you think the three chickens died?

5. Why do you think the parrot wouldn't say "Cataño?"

Referents/Antecedents

1. "There was no *other* like him" (paragraph 1). No other what?

   _____

2. "Why can't you say that *one word*?" (paragraph 2). What one word?_____

3. "The bird would never repeat *the name*" (paragraph 2). What name? _____

4. "He was shocked by *what he saw*" (paragraph 5). What did he see? _____

5. "The parrot was screaming at the *fourth* (paragraph 6). The fourth what? _____

Topics for Writing/Discussion

○ What do you know about the character of the man?
○ What do you know about the character of the parrot?
○ Have you ever been stubborn and refused to do something that you could do? Tell about it.
○ Do you know any other story about a unique bird? Tell it.
○ Rewrite this story from the point of view of the parrot.
○ Rewrite this story from the point of view of the man.

The Story of the Smart Parrot

Nolbu and Hyungbu: The Story of Two Brothers

Before you start to read

○ Do you know any stories in your language about brothers or sisters in which the younger one is favored or rewarded for being a good person?

○ In this story about two brothers, the younger one is honest, kind and poor. His older brother, on the other hand, is selfish and rich. Read the story to find out how each brother gets what he deserves.

○ Do you know any stories in which a kind person helped an animal and then the animal helped the person?

○ Stop at the end of paragraph 5. What do you think Nolbu will do?

○ Stop after paragraph 6. What do you think will happen when Nolbu opens his gourd?

○ Stop after paragraph 7. What do you think Hyungbu will do when his older brother comes to him for help?

Nolbu and Hyungbu: The Story of Two Brothers

Nolbu and Hyungbu: the Story of Two Brothers

1   A long time ago, there were two brothers, Nolbu and Hyungbu. Nolbu, the older brother, was rich and greedy. Hyungbu, the younger brother, was the opposite. He was poor and generous.

2   One day Hyungbu's seven children were so hungry that they were going to die. Hyungbu decided to ask his brother for some rice. But Nolbu's wife didn't want to give him any rice. She hit him in the face with the rice spoon. Hyungbu was so hungry that he took the little bit of rice on his face and ate it! Then he asked her to hit his face on the other side. This time the sister-in-law hit him with a clean spoon.

3   On his way home, Hyungbu found a swallow with a broken leg. He took care of the bird. Then he let it fly away.

4   The next spring the swallow brought a gourd seed to Hyungbu. Hyungbu planted it in the ground, and in the autumn he had many gourds.

5   When he cut open the gourds, pieces of gold fell out. After that he became very rich and lived in a big house. His greedy brother came to him and asked, "How can you be so rich?" Hyungbu told him the truth.

6   After Nolbu left Hyungbu's house, he found a swallow. He broke the swallow's leg. Then he took care of it. When the bird was well again, he let it fly away. The next year the swallow brought him a gourd seed. He planted it in the spring, and in the fall he harvested it.

7   When Nolbu opened the gourd, dirty water came out. The water covered his house and his farm. Suddenly he became a poor man. He had nothing to eat and no place to sleep.

8   He went to Hyungbu's house and asked for help. Good Hyungbu gave him food to eat and a warm place to sleep.

9   Then Nolbu understood his mistakes. He decided to be a good brother. They lived happily together for the rest of their lives.

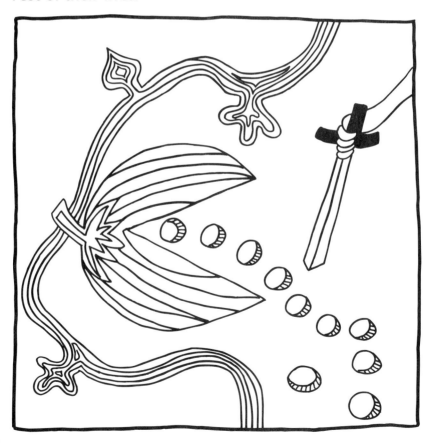

Exercises

Matching

Match the word in column 1 with the word that means the opposite (antonym) in column two.

1. _____ rich
2. _____ autumn
3. _____ greedy
4. _____ younger
5. _____ broke
6. _____ plant
7. _____ truth

a. older
b. fall
c. spring
d. poor
e. harvest
f. fixed
g. lie
h. generous

Comprehension

1. What words were used to start this story?
2. What words at the end mean the same as "they lived happily ever after"?
3. What is the subject of the first sentence? What is the verb?
4. How many children did Hyungbu have?
5. What did Nolbu's wife do when Hyungbu asked her for food?
6. What did the swallow bring Hyungbu? Why did the swallow help him?
7. What was inside Hyungbu's gourd?.
8. What was inside Nolbu's gourd?
9. Was Nolbu a nice person? How do you know?
10. Was Hyungbu a nice person? How do you know?
11. What kind of animal is a swallow? What clues in paragraph 3 help you guess the answer?

Past Tense Review

Some of the following verbs are regular. They take the *ed* ending. Others are irregular. Write the past tense for these verbs.

Present tense	Past tense
1. are	_____
2. do	_____
3. hit	_____
4. eat	_____
5. find	_____
6. plant	_____
7. bring	_____
8. let	_____
9. harvest	_____
10. break	_____
11. help	_____
12. tell	_____
13. become	_____
14. take	_____
15. cut	_____
16. leave	_____
17. open	_____
18. cover	_____
19. understand	_____
20. give	_____

True–False

1. _____ Nolbu broke a swallow's leg.
2. _____ Hyungbu had five children.
3. _____ Nolbu's wife hit Hyungbu with a spoon.
4. _____ Nolbu's gourds were filled with dirty water.
5. _____ Hyungbu became rich.
6. _____ Hyungbu was a good person.
7. _____ Hyungbu helped his brother when Nolbu was poor.
8. _____ Nolbu helped his brother when Hyungbu was poor.
9. _____ Hyungbu helped a swallow with a broken leg.
10. _____ In the spring Hyungbu had many gourds.

Reading from Context

1. On his way home, he found a *swallow* with a broken wing. He took care of the bird. What is a *swallow*?
2. Nolbu was rich and *greedy*. He always wanted more money for himself and he never helped other people. What is *greedy*?
3. Hyungbu was *generous*. He gave his brother food and money. What does *generous* mean?
4. Nolbu was rich and greedy. Hyungbu was the *opposite*. He was poor and generous. What is the meaning of *opposite*?
5. Hyungbu told his brother the truth. *Truth* means:
   a. a lie
   b. a real reason
   c. a question
   d. a story
6. His *sister-in-law* hit him with a rice spoon. A sister-in-law is:
   a. your mother's daughter
   b. your sister's daughter
   c. the woman your brother marries
   d. the woman you marry
   e. your sister

Sentence Order

Put these sentences in the correct order.

1. _____ Hyungbu asked his sister-in-law for rice.

2. _____ Nolbu broke the swallow's leg.

3. _____ Hyungbu's children were very hungry.

4. _____ Hyungbu opened a gourd and gold fell out.

5. _____ Nolbu became a poor man.

6. _____ A swallow brought Hyungbu a gourd seed.

7. _____ Nolbu planted his gourd seed.

8. _____ Hyungbu gave his brother food and a place to sleep.

Idiom Practice

There is a phrase in English: "to turn the other cheek." It means to refuse to fight, to accept pain instead of fighting back. What sentence in paragraph 2 gives an example of turning the other cheek?

N olbu and H yungbu: the S tory of T wo B rothers

1   Once there were two brothers. Although Nolbu, the older one, was rich and greedy, Hyungbu, the younger brother, was poor and generous.

2   One day when Hyungbu's seven children were starving, he went to ask his brother for rice to feed them. But when his sister-in-law saw Hyungbu, she did not want to give him any rice. Instead she hit him on the cheek with the rice scoop. Hyungbu was so hungry that he ate the little bit of rice on his face. Then he turned the other cheek and told her to hit him again. This time she hit him with a clean scoop.

3   On his way home, Hyungbu found a swallow whose leg was broken. He took care of it until it was well, and then let it fly away.

4   When spring came, the swallow brought Hyungbu a gourd seed to plant. In the fall, after he harvested the gourds, Hyungbu opened one of them. Gold coins poured out! Then he became a rich man.

5   Nolbu was jealous because his younger brother now had a big house with a beautiful garden. He wanted to know how Hyungbu became so rich. So Hyungbu told him exactly what had happened.

6   On the way home from Hyungbu's house, Nolbu found a swallow. He broke its leg, and then cared for it. After it got better, he let it fly away. The following year, the swallow brought him a gourd seed. Nolbu did just what Hyungbu had done.

7   But, in the autumn, when Nolbu opened his gourd, there was no gold. Instead dirty water poured out of it. The water flooded his house and farm. Suddenly he was a poor man with no food and no roof!

8   Nolbu didn't know what to do. He begged Hyungbu for help, and of course his kind brother said yes.

9   Then Nolbu understood his own faults. He made up his mind to be a better person. He, his brother, and their families lived together happily for the rest of their lives.

Exercises

Matching

Match the words in the first column with their definitions in the second column.

1. _____ made up one's mind   a. a kind of spoon

2. _____ scoop   b. next

3. _____ roof   c. always wanting to
                                       have more things or
                                       money

4. _____ suddenly   d. very, very hungry

5. _____ following   e. willing to give
                                       to others

6. _____ starving   f. flow or spill steadily

7. _____ harvested   g. upset about what
                                       another person has

8. _____ faults   h. the top of the house

9. _____ pour   i. decided

10. _____ jealous   j. mistakes, bad habits

11. _____ greedy   k. asked for, pleaded for

12. _____ begged   l. picked crops

13. _____ generous   m. covered with water

14. _____ flooded   n. quickly, without
                                       warning

15. _____ gourd   o. took

                                     p. fruit with a hard shell

Comprehension

1. Paragraph 5 says, "Hyungbu told him exactly what had happened." What did Hyungbu tell him about?
2. Paragraph 6 says, "Nolbu did just what Hyungbu had done." What had Hyungbu done?
3. "Suddenly, he was a poor man with no food and no roof." (paragraph 7) This means:
   a. his house lost its roof
   b. his house was destroyed
   c. his roof was wet
   d. his house didn't have a roof

4. Circle the words that describe Nolbu at the beginning of the story.

generous	**greedy**	**rich**
poor	**mean**	**selfish**

5. Circle the words that describe Hyungbu at the beginning of the story.

hungry	**poor**	**rich**	**generous**
selfish	**greedy**	**kind**	

6. Circle the words that describe Nolbu's wife?

married	**single**	**generous**	**greedy**	**selfish**
considerate	**impolite**	**mean**	**rich**	

7. Circle the words that describe Hyungbu at the end of the story.

hungry	**poor**	**rich**	**generous**
kind	**selfish**	**greedy**	

8. Circle the words that describe Nolbu near the end of the story.

poor	**rich**	**married**	**single**
sorry	**angry**	**greedy**	**nicer**

9. Why do you think the swallow gave Hyungbu a gourd seed that would grow gold-filled gourds and Nolbu a seed that grew water-filled gourds?

Vocabulary from Context

1. Which word in paragraph 1 means the opposite of "generous"?

   _____

2. Which word in paragraph 2 means "hungry"?

   _____

3. Which word in paragraph 2 means "side of the face"?

   _____

4. Which word in paragraph 2 means "big spoon or ladle"?

   _____

5. Which word in paragraph 3 means "a kind of bird"?

   _____

6. Which word in paragraph 4 means "picked ripe fruits or vegetables"? _____

7. What phrase in paragraph 5 means "just what had taken place"? _____

8. Which phrase in paragraph 6 means "look after, nurse, tend"?

   _____

9. What phrase in paragraph 6 means "did the same thing as"?

   _____

10. What word in paragraph 7 means the same as "fall" in paragraph 4? _____

11. Which phrase in paragraph 9 means "decided"?

    _____

Dictionary Skills

Define the following underlined words as they are used in the sentence.

1. The <u>following</u> spring, the swallow brought him a gourd seed.

   definition _____

   part of speech _____

2. Please stop <u>following</u> me, or I will call the police.

   definition _____

   part of speech _____

3. The following <u>spring</u>, the swallow brought him a gourd seed.

   definition _____

   part of speech _____

4. The <u>spring</u> in my mattress is broken.

   definition _____

   part of speech _____

5. The following spring, the <u>swallow</u> brought him a gourd seed.

   definition _____

   part of speech _____

6. Because she had a sore throat, it hurt her to <u>swallow</u> any food.

   definition _____

   part of speech _____

7. In the <u>fall</u>, he harvested the gourds.

   definition _____

   part of speech _____

8. Don't let the baby <u>fall</u> into the water.

   definition _____

   part of speech _____

Analogies

Analogies are comparisons. To do analogies, decide on the relationship between the first two things and then find two other things that have the same relationship.

Circle the comparison that has the same relationship as the sample. Use your dictionary for words you don't know.

Example: *Big* is to *little* as

    a. *old* is to *new*.

    b. *old* is to *elderly*.

    c. *big* is to *large*.

The answer is *a.* because *big* is the opposite of *little* and *old* is the opposite of *new*.

Example: *Apple* is to *fruit* as

    a. *orange* is to *pear*

    b. *carrot* is to *vegetable*

    c. *fruit* is to *vegetable*

The answer is *b.* because *apple* is a kind of *fruit* and *carrot* is a kind of *vegetable*.

1. *Rich* is to *poor* as
   a. *generous* is to *kind*
   b. *generous* is to *greedy*
   c. greedy is to *selfish*

2. *Swallow* is to *bird* as
   a. *gourd* is to *gold*
   b. *gourd* is to *fruit*
   c. *gourd* is to *harvest*

3. *Autumn* is to *fall* as
   a. *spring* is to *winter*
   b. *happy* is to *glad*
   c. *harvest* is to *gourd*.

4. *Plant* is to *harvest* as
   a. *sow* is to *reap*
   b. *big* is to *large*
   c. *pour* is to *flood*

Sentence Combining

Use the word in parentheses to combine each set of sentences. Sometimes you will have to leave words out of the combined sentence.

1. Nolbu was rich and greedy. Hyungbu was poor and generous.

    (although) _____

2. Hyungbu found a swallow. Its leg was broken.

    (whose) _____

3. Hyungbu harvested the gourds. He opened one.

    (after) _____

4. Nolbu was jealous. His younger brother now had a big house.

    (because) _____

5. His younger brother had a big house. It had a garden.

    (with) _____

6. Nolbu opened his gourd. There was no gold in it.

    (when) _____

7. Suddenly he was a poor man. He had no food and no roof.

    (with) _____

Apposition

A phrase that comes after another and means the same person or thing is an *appositive phrase*.

> **Example:** Nolbu, *the older brother*, was rich and greedy.

> The older brother is the same person as Nolbu, so that is an appositive phrase.

Example: She hit Hyungbu with a rice scoop, *a kind of ladle or spoon*. "A kind of ladle or spoon" means the same as rice scoop so the italicized phrase is an appositive.

In the following sentences, underline the appositive phrase.

1. Gourds, fruits with hard shells, are popular at Halloween.
2. Hyungbu, the younger brother, was kind and poor.
3. Autumn, the season when the leaves change, is a beautiful time of year.

Topics for Discussion

○ "Make up one's mind" means to decide. Nolbu made up his mind to be a better person. Can you think of an example of something you made up your mind to do?

○ There are many stories in which the younger brother is nicer or smarter than the older one. Tell one of these stories that you know.

○ Can you think of any other stories where a person helps an animal and then the animal helps the person?

○ If you were Nyungbu, would you help your brother Nolbu? Why or why not?

○ What kind of person was Hyungbu at the beginning of the story? What kind of person was Nolbu? How did they change? Why?

○ What other story in this book tells about greed? Are those two stories alike in any way? How are they different?

BETEL AND ARECA

Before you start to read

○ Do you know anyone who loved someone so much that he/she was willing to give his/her life for the other's happiness?

○ Some wedding customs are so old that people have forgotten how or why they started. Read this story to find out about the beginning of a wedding tradition that many Vietnamese people still follow.

○ In different cultures there are different beliefs about the importance of love of family and marital love. Which bond— the bond of blood (family) or the bond of marriage—is stronger in your culture?

○ Read this story. Does one kind of love seem stronger than the other in this story?

206   Betel and Areca

Betel and Areca

1   Once upon a time, there was a family with two sons. The parents died, and the two brothers lived together. They looked alike, and they loved each other very much.

2   After the older brother got married, his wife often got mixed up because they were so much alike. The brothers were sad about this.

3   The younger brother wanted his older brother to be happy, so he went away to the forest and he died there. When he died, he turned into a limestone rock.

4   The older brother felt sad and lonely. He wanted to see his brother, so he went to look for him in the forest. He saw the limestone rock and sat down on it. Then he died, too. After he died, he turned into an areca tree.

5   When the wife went to the forest to look for the brothers, she saw the rock and the tree. Then she died too. She became a betel vine. The vine climbed around the areca tree.

6   After that, people saw the three things together, the limestone rock, the areca tree and the betel vine. They ate the fruit from the areca tree and the leaf from the betel vine with the powder from the limestone.

7   The king heard about this and he decided to make it a custom: When people get married, they chew these three things together.

Exercises

Pronoun Reference
Which words or ideas do the underlined pronouns refer to?

1. "<u>They</u> looked alike. (paragraph 1) _____

2. "The brothers were sad about <u>this</u>. (paragraph 2)

   _____

3. "<u>He</u> saw the limestone rock and sat down on <u>it</u>." (paragraph 4)

   he _____ it _____

4. "People saw <u>these three things together</u>." (paragraph 6)

   1. _____ 2. _____ 3. _____

5. "The king heard about <u>this</u>, and he decided to make <u>it</u> a
   custom." (paragraph 7)

   this _____ he_____ it _____

6. "They chew <u>these three things together</u>." (paragraph 7)

   1. _____ 2. _____ 3. _____

Comprehension
1. Why did the wife get mixed up?
2. Why did the younger brother leave the house and go
   to the forest?
3. What did the younger brother become when he died?
4. Who became a betel vine?
5. What custom did the king start?
6. What three things do people chew when they get married?

True–False

1. _____ The younger brother left because he didn't like his sister-in-law.
2. _____ The older brother got married.
3. _____ The younger brother turned into an areca tree.
4. _____ When the wife died, she became a betel vine.
5. _____ The brothers loved each other.
6. _____ When people get married they chew the fruit from the areca tree, the leaf of the betel vine and the powder from the limestone.
7. _____ The betel vine climbs around the areca tree.
8. _____ The brothers were twins.

Sentence Order

1. _____ The vine climbed around the areca tree.
2. _____ The king decided to make it a custom for people to eat these three things when they marry.
3. _____ The parents died.
4. _____ The younger brother went to the forest.
5. _____ The older brother died.
6. _____ The older brother got married.
7. _____ The wife died and became a betel vine.
8. _____ The older brother felt sad and lonely.

Matching

Match the words in the first column with their definitions in the
second column.

1. _____ alike   a. to care about

2. _____ chew   b. confused

3. _____ forest   c. to put together

4. _____ lonely   d. a climbing plant

5. _____ mixed up   e. finely ground
                                          pieces

6. _____ powder   f. the same

7. _____ vine   g. grind with
                                          the teeth

8. _____ custom   h. a sad feeling of
                                          being alone

                                          i. trees, woods

                                          j. usual habit,
                                          tradition

Sentence Combining

Use the word in parentheses to combine each pair of sentences.

1. The older brother got married. His wife often got mixed up.

   (after) _____

2. His wife got mixed up. The brothers looked alike.

   (because) _____

3. He died. He turned into a limestone rock.

   (when) _____

Betel and Areca

1   Once upon a time, there were two orphaned brothers who lived together. They looked almost identical, and they loved each other very much.

B

2   After the older brother got married, his wife often confused the two brothers because they were so similar. This made both of the brothers sad.

3   The younger brother wanted his older brother to be happy, so he went away to the forest. There he died and turned into a limestone rock.

4   The older brother felt lonely and missed his sibling. He went to the forest to search for him. He came to the limestone rock and sat down on it. Then he, too, died. After he died, he turned into an areca tree.

5   When the wife went to the woods to look for the brothers, she saw the rock and the tree. Then she died, too. She became a betel vine, climbing around the areca tree.

6   After that, people saw the three things together. They tasted the fruit from the areca tree and the leaf from the betel vine with the powder from the limestone. When they chewed these things, their teeth became strong.

7   When the king heard of this custom, he wrote a decree. From then on, when people wanted to marry, they would chew these three things together.

Exercises

Comprehension

1. *From then on* means:
    a. alike
    b. when
    c. after that time
    d. in the past

2. There were two orphaned brothers.
    a. What is the subject of that sentence? _____
    b. What is the verb? _____

3. What phrase is used to start the story?

    _____

4. The king made his decree because:
    a. he wanted his people to have strong teeth.
    b. this was the people's custom anyway.
    c. he wanted a marriage custom that represented love and devotion.

5. "When the king heard of *this custom* . . ." (paragraph 7). What custom? _____

6. "He made a decree." What was the king's decree?

    _____

Vocabulary

Choose from the following words to fill in the blanks:

alike   chewed   climbing   confused   decreed
miss   orphaned   similar   tasted

1. The boys were _____ when their parents died in a fire.

2. Alex _____ the meat for a long time because it was tough.

3. The homework assignment was so difficult that Alan got _____.

4. My new car is _____ to yours.

5. Jon and Ricky were _____ the mountain when they got hurt.

6. We _____ our friends when we don't see them for a long time.

Reading from Context

1. What word in paragraph 1 means "without parents"?

   _____

2. What word in paragraph 1 means "exactly alike"?

   _____

3. What word in paragraph 2 means "almost identical or somewhat alike"? _____

4. What word in paragraph 5 means the same as "forest"?

   _____

5. What word in paragraph 6 means "to use the teeth to eat"?

_____

6. What word in paragraph 7 means "a habit, an accepted social practice"? _____

7. What word in paragraph 7 means "an official order or law"?

_____

8. What word in paragraph 4 means "brother or sister"?

_____

9. What word in paragraph 5 means "a climbing plant"?

_____

Sentence Combining

Use the words in parentheses to combine each pair of sentences.

1. There were two orphaned brothers. They lived together.
   (who) _____

2. He died. He turned into an areca tree.
   (after) _____

3. The wife went to the woods to look for the brothers. She saw the rock and the tree.
   (when) _____

4. She became a betel vine. The betel vine was climbing around the areca tree.
   (leave out some words) _____

5. They chewed these things. Their teeth became strong.
   (when) _____

Topics for Discussion/Writing

○ In this story it is a custom to eat limestone powder, areca fruit, and betel leaves at weddings. Weddings are a time to express love. Why would these foods be appropriate for a wedding?

○ What is a common wedding custom in your country? Do you know how it started or what it means?

○ Was the younger brother right or wrong in his decision to leave the house? Why do you think so?

○ There are different kinds of love—brotherly love and marital love. Give an example of both kinds of love in this story.

THE GOLDEN AX

Before you start to read

○ This is a story about a good younger brother and a bad older brother. As you read this story, think about the similarities and differences between this story and "Nolbu and Hyungbu."

○ Discuss the saying "Honesty is the best policy." What does it mean? As you read the story think about which brother follows that saying and which one does not.

○ Stop at the end of paragraph 6. Write or discuss your own ending to the story.

The Golden Ax

THE GOLDEN AX

1   A long time ago, two brothers lived in a small village. The younger brother was Li Gang, and the older brother was Li Ping.

2   Every morning the brothers crossed over a small river to go to work. One morning when Li Gang crossed the bridge, his ax fell into the river. He sat down and cried.

3   Suddenly he saw an old man in front of him. The old man asked him why he was crying. Li Gang said, "I dropped my ax into the water and now I cannot work." Then the old man went away.

4   Soon he returned with a silver ax. Li Gang looked at it and said, "That is not my ax." Then the man brought another ax. It was made of gold. But Li Gang said it was not his ax.

5   Finally the old man showed him an iron ax. Li Gang said, "That is the ax I lost." The old man said, "You are an honest boy. I will give you your ax and the gold ax, too."

6   When Li Gang got home, he told his brother about the man and the axes. But his brother could hardly believe it. So the next morning Li Pilng went to the river and dropped his ax from the bridge. Then he started to cry loudly.

7   The old man came. Li Ping told him that he had dropped his ax. Li Ping asked for help.

8   When the old man brought the silver ax to him, Li Ping said that it was his. Then the old man showed him the golden ax. He said that the golden ax was also his.

9   But the old man was unhappy. He said, "You are not an honest boy. You cannot keep the silver ax or the golden ax. And I will not return your iron ax." Then he went away.

Exercises

Antonyms

Match the word in the first column with the word that means the *opposite* in the second column.

1. _____ village
2. _____ bridge
3. _____ drop
4. _____ suddenly
5. _____ finally
6. _____ honest
7. _____ unhappy

  a. pick up
  b. slowly
  c. immediately
  d. big city
  e. untrustworthy
  f. truthful
  g. tunnel
  h. glad
  i. at last

True–False

1. _____ Li Gang was the older brother.
2. _____ Li Ping was an honest boy.
3. _____ Li Ping dropped a silver ax.
4. _____ Li Ping dropped his ax down a mountain.
5. _____ At the end of the story, Li Ping didn't have any axes.
6. _____ Li Ping dropped his ax by accident.
7. _____ Li Gang dropped his ax by accident.
8. _____ The old man gave Li Gang a golden ax.

Comprehension

1. Why did the old man show Li Ping a golden ax?
2. Why did the old man give Li Gang a golden ax?
3. Why did Li Gang need an ax?
4. Where did the ax fall?
5. Why did the old man say that Li Ping was not an honest boy?
6. Who was the honest boy?

Sentence Order

Put the sentences in the correct order.

1. _____ Li Gang dropped his ax.

2. _____ Li Ping dropped his ax.

3. _____ Li Gang saw an old man in front of him.

4. _____ Li Ping told the old man the silver ax was his.

5. _____ The man gave Li Gang a golden ax.

Sentence Combining

Use the word or instructions in parentheses to combine each pair of sentences.

1. Suddenly he saw an old man. The old man was in front of him.

   (leave out words) _____

2. Every morning the brothers crossed a bridge. The bridge went over a small river.

   (leave out words) _____

3. Li Gang crossed the bridge. His ax fell into the river.

   (when) _____

4. Li Gang got home. He told his brother about the man and the axes.
   (when) _____

5. The old man brought an ax. It was made of silver.
   (leave out words) _____

Pronoun Reference

Tell who or what the underlined words refer to.

1. "The two brothers crossed a bridge." (paragraph 2)

   _____

2. "He sat down and cried." (paragraph 2)

   _____

3. "Li Gang looked at it and said, "That is not my ax."" (paragraph 4)

   it _____   that _____

4. "But his brother did not believe it." (paragraph 6)

   his _____   it _____

5. "Then he went away." (paragraph 9)

   _____

Matching

Match the words in the first column with the definitions in the second column.

1. _____ village
2. _____ drop
3. _____ ax
4. _____ honest
5. _____ bridge
6. _____ finally
7. _____ suddenly
8. _____ cross

a. quickly and unexpectedly
b. small town
c. go from one side to the other
d. polite
e. tool for cutting wood
f. let fall
g. at last
h. a span or crossway over a river, railway, etc.
i. truthful

THE GOLDEN AX

1   A long time ago, two brothers lived together in a small village. The younger brother was called Li Gang, and the older brother was called Li Ping.

2   Every morning on their way to work, the brothers had to cross a bridge over a small river. One morning as Li Gang was crossing the bridge, he dropped his ax into the water by accident. He sat down and started to cry because he could not work without his ax.

3   Suddenly an old man appeared in front of him and asked why he was crying. After Li Gang explained what had happened, the old man disappeared. When he returned, he was carrying a silver ax. Li Gang looked at it and said that it was not his. Then the old man brought another ax that was made of gold. But Li Gang said that one wasn't his either.

4   Finally the old man brought the old iron ax. Li Gang said, "Yes, that's it. That's the ax I lost." The old man told him that because he was an honest boy, he could have not only his own ax but also the gold ax.

5   When Li Gang got home, he told his brother what happened, but his brother could hardly believe the story.

So the next morning, Li Ping went to the bridge and dropped his ax into the water on purpose. Then he began to weep loudly.

6   Soon the old man came. Li Ping explained what had happened and asked the old man for his help.

7   When the old man brought him the silver ax, Li Ping said it was his, and when the old man brought the golden ax, Li Ping said that it was his also. "You are dishonest. You cannot have either of these axes, and I will not give back your iron ax," the old man said. Then he disappeared.

Exercises

Matching

Match the word in the first column with a word in the second column that means the *opposite*. (*antonym*)

1. _____ appeared
2. _____ returned
3. _____ by accident
4. _____ loudly
5. _____ dropped
6. _____ younger
7. _____ honest
8. _____ weep

a. seemed
b. left
c. happily
d. disappeared
e. on purpose
f. newer
g. older
h. softly
i. picked up
j. cry
k. laugh
l. dishonest

Fill-in-the Blanks

Choose from the following words to fill in the blanks.

ax	bridge	explained	finally	golden
honest	on purpose	suddenly	village	

1. I _____ the problem to my friend.
2. The people lived in a small _____, not a big city.
3. The man used an _____ to cut down the tree.
4. We had to cross the _____ to get over the river.
5. We waited and waited until our friend _____ arrived.

Vocabulary Development—
Synonyms and Antonyms

One word in each group has a different meaning than the other words.
Circle the word that is different. Use the dictionary to help with
unfamiliar words.

1. laugh   cry   weep   sob

2. dishonest   trustworthy   truthful   honest

3. accidentally unintentionally on purpose by accident

4. disappeared came   left   went away

5. village   hamlet   small town   city

Dictionary Skills

Define the underlined words as they are used in the sentences.

1. The priest wore a <u>cross</u> around his neck.

   definition _____

   part of speech _____

2. The child was not allowed to <u>cross</u> the street alone.

   definition _____

   part of speech _____

3. Olga was tired and <u>cross</u> this morning.

   definition _____

   part of speech _____

4. John lost two teeth in the car accident, so the dentist made him
   a <u>bridge</u>.

   definition _____

   part of speech _____

5. Sandy and her friends play <u>bridge</u> every Saturday.

   definition _____

   part of speech _____

6. I prefer to take the <u>bridge</u> instead of the tunnel when I have to cross the river.

   definition _____

   part of speech _____

7. Lana <u>dropped</u> her glass and it broke.

   definition _____

   part of speech _____

8. Alan had to <u>drop</u> two classes this semester.

   definition _____

   part of speech _____

9. The ballgame was canceled when the first <u>drop</u> of rain came.

   definition _____

   part of speech _____

10. The ax was made of <u>iron</u>.

    definition _____

    part of speech _____

11. Mark decided to <u>iron</u> the clothes and surprise his wife.

    definition _____

    part of speech _____

Comprehension

1. "Li Gang explained *what had happened*" (paragraph 3). What had happened? Who did he explain it to?
2. "Li Gang looked at *it* and said that *it* was not his" (paragraph 3). What wasn't his?
3. Li Gang said *that one* wasn't his either" (paragraph 3). What does "that one" refer to?
4. Which brother dropped his ax by accident? Which one dropped his on purpose?
5. Which brother was honest?
6. Why didn't the old man give Li Ping his ax?
7. The old man told him that because he was an honest boy, he could have not only his own ax but also the gold ax. This means:

   a. he could not have his own ax or the gold ax.

   b. he could not have the gold ax.

   c. he could only have his ax.

   d. he could have both his ax and the gold ax.

Review of Direct and Indirect Speech.

Change the underlined part of the following sentences to direct speech. See the review at the end of story 1 if you forget how to do this.

1. Li Gang looked at the ax and said <u>that it was not his</u>.

   _____

2. When the old man showed him the golden ax, Li Ping said <u>that it was his also</u>.

   _____

3. The old man told him <u>that because he was an honest boy, he could have not only his ax but also the gold ax</u>.

   _____

Change the following sentences from direct speech to indirect speech.

4. "You are dishonest," the old man said to Li Ping.

_____

5. Li Gang said to the old man, "That's the ax I lost."

_____

Topics for Discussion

○ How is this story similar to "Nolbu and Hyungbu"? How is Li Ping like Nolbu? How is Li Gang like Hyungbu?
○ Many stories have a moral or lesson that they teach. This story teaches that "Honesty is the best policy." Do you know any stories from your country that teach the same lesson?
○ What other stories in this book teach the same lesson?

THE LION AND THE HYENA

Before you start to read

○ Did you ever have a friend who was bigger and stronger than you? How did you settle arguments when you and that friend disagreed?

○ What are some good ways to settle disagreements among friends?

○ The lion is often called "the king of the jungle" or "the king of the animals." When you read the story, decide whether you think the hyena or the lion is right. Decide why most of the animals said the lion was right.

1.

2.

The Lion and the Hyena

The Lion and the Hyena

1   A long time ago, the lion was the king of the animals. He and the hyena were friends. They often went out to look for food together.

2   One day they found a cow and a bull. The lion said to the hyena, "You can have the cow. I want the bull because it's powerful like me." The hyena was afraid of the lion, so he said yes.

3   The lion was very busy being king, so the hyena took care of the cow and the bull. One day the hyena said to the lion, "My cow will soon have a baby." When the baby cow was born, the lion went to look at it. "This isn't your cow's baby; it's my bull's baby!" said the lion to the hyena. Then the two friends disagreed.

4   They called all the old and wise animals to decide who owned the baby cow. All the animals came except the ape. They all said that the baby cow belonged to the lion. But as they were leaving, the ape finally arrived. "I was very busy," he said to the lion.

5   The lion shouted, "I'm king of the animals, and I'm here! Why were you too busy to come?" "I was sewing the earth and the sky together," the ape explained. Then the lion asked, "How is it possible to sew the earth and sky together?" "First tell me," the ape answered, "how is it possible for a bull to have a baby?"

Exercises

Sentence Order

Put these sentences in the correct order.

1. _____ The lion and the hyena found a bull and a cow.

2. _____ The ape explained why he was late.

3. _____ All the wise animals met to decide who owned the baby cow.

4. _____ The lion said he wanted the bull because it was strong.

5. _____ A baby cow was born.

Comprehension

1. Why did the lion want the bull?
2. Why did the hyena let the lion have the bull?
3. Who took care of the bull and the cow?
4. How did the lion and hyena decide who owned the baby cow?
5. Why did the ape say he was late?
6. In this story:
   a. which animal was wise?
   b. which one took care of his animals?
   c. which one was a "bully"?
   d. which animals were strong?
   e. which animal had a baby?
   f. which animal was the leader of the animals?

Matching

Match the words in the first column with their definitions in the second column.

1. _____ belonged
2. _____ possible
3. _____ hyena
4. _____ arrived
5. _____ powerful

6. _____ disagreed
7. _____ bull

8. _____ sew
9. _____ wise

a. was owned by
b. can happen
c. strong
d. argued
e. intelligent, having good sense, understanding

f. a male cow
g. to stitch together with needle and thread

h. came
i. a wild doglike animal

Inferences

Inferences are things that can be learned from a reading even though they are not stated in the reading.

1. Do you think the ape was really sewing the sky and earth together?
2. Why do you think he said that?
3. Why did the other animals want to give the baby cow to the lion?
4. Did the ape want to give the baby cow to the lion or the hyena?
5. Who gave birth to the baby? Who was the baby's father?

Word Forms

Prefix *dis-*. In other readings, the prefix *dis-*, meaning *bad, wrong, not*, appeared in the words *dishonest* and *disappear*. In this story, there is the word *disagree*. How many other words beginning with *dis-* (meaning *wrong, bad,* or *not*) can you find?

Choose from the following forms to fill in the blanks

disagree   **disagreement**   **disagrees**
disagreed   **disagreeable**

1. Mary and John always _____ about which movie to see.

2. Martha always _____ with everyone; she is a _____ person.

3. The lion and the hyena _____ about who owned the baby cow, so they called a meeting of the wise animals.

4. It is possible to _____ without being

   _____.

5. The lion and the hyena had a _____ about the ownership of the baby cow.

Use three of the words above to write three true sentences.

_____

_____

_____

Pronoun Reference

Tell what word, words, or ideas the underlined words refer to.

1. I want the bull because it is powerful like me.

   I _____ it _____ me _____

2. This isn't your cow's baby; it's my bull's baby.

   this _____ it _____

3. The two friends disagreed.

   _____

4. As they were leaving, the ape finally arrived.

   _____

True–False

1. _____ The hyena wanted to give the bull to the lion.
2. _____ The hyena took care of both the bull and the cow.
3. _____ The ape sewed the sky and earth together.
4. _____ The animals said the baby cow belonged to the lion.
5. _____ The bull gave birth to a baby.
6. _____ The lion was strong.
7. _____ The lion was king of the animals.
8. _____ The lion and the hyena were friends.
9. _____ The cow gave birth to a baby.
10. _____ The ape thought that the hyena should keep the baby cow.

THE LION AND THE HYENA

1   Long ago the lion, the king of the beasts, and the hyena were good friends. Often they went together to search for food. **B**

2   One day while the two friends were out, they found a cow and a bull. The lion said, "You can have the cow. I will take the bull, which is powerful like me." The hyena agreed because he was afraid of the lion.

3   After a while the cow gave birth to a calf. The two friends fought over the calf; each claimed that it belonged to him.

4   Finally they called all the wise animals to judge who was right. When all the animals but the ape had gathered together, they decided that the lion owned the new calf. But just as they were getting ready to leave, the ape came. He apologized for being late. "I was very busy," he told the lion.

5   "Why were you so busy"? shouted the lion. "I was stitching the earth and sky together," the ape explained. Then the lion asked, "How is that possible"? "First tell me," the ape replied, "how is it possible for a bull to have a baby?"

Exercises

Matching

Match the words in the first column with their definitions in the second column.

1. _____ claimed
2. _____ shouted
3. _____ beast
4. _____ apologized
5. _____ gathered
6. _____ calf
7. _____ search
8. _____ stitching
9. _____ judge
10. _____ agree
11. _____ bull
12. _____ powerful
13. _____ belong to
14. _____ replied
15. _____ hyena
16. _____ but

a. wild, doglike animal
b. answered
c. be owned by
d. strong
e. came together
f. yelled
g. talk
h. wild animal
i. said "I'm sorry"
j. sewing
k. fixing
l. except
m. maybe
n. look for
o. a baby cow
p. to decide
q. to have the same opinion
r. said something was true
s. male cow

Dictionary Use

Define the underlined word as it is used in the sentence.

1. Nikki has her <u>own</u> car.

   definition _____

   part of speech _____

2. Bobby <u>owns</u> two dogs.

   definition _____

   part of speech _____

3. The king almost drowned because he got a <u>stitch</u> in his side while he was swimming.

   definition _____

   part of speech _____

4. The ape said that he <u>stitched</u> the sky and earth together.

   definition _____

   part of speech _____

5. Tom sat in the dark because the <u>power</u> was out in his neighborhood.

   definition _____

   part of speech _____

6. The lion is a very strong animal; he has a lot of <u>power</u>.

   definition _____

   part of speech _____

Sentence Combining

Use the words or instructions in parentheses to combine the sentences.

1. The lion was the king of beasts. The lion and the hyena were friends.

   (leave out words) _____

2. I'll take the bull. It's powerful like me.

   (which) _____

3. They were getting ready to leave. The ape came.

   (just as) _____

4. All the animals gathered. They decided the calf belonged to the lion.

   (when) _____

5. The hyena agreed. He was afraid of the lion.

   (because) _____

6. They went together. They searched for food.

   (use the infinitive) _____

Transition Words

When stories are told in chronological (time) order, certain words are used for transition (movement from one part of the story to the next). The following words are used to set up time relationships in this story.

long ago   **one day**   **after a while**   **finally**   **then**

Look to see where each of these words was used in the story.

Referents

In each sentence, tell what the underlined words or phrases refer to.

1. "The lion, <u>the king of beasts</u>, and the hyena were friends."
   (paragraph 1) _____

2. "<u>The two friends</u> fought over the calf; <u>each</u> claimed <u>it</u> belonged
   to him." (paragraph 3)

   the two friends _____

   each _____

   it _____

3. "But just as <u>they</u> were getting ready to leave, the ape came."
   (paragraph 4) _____

Topics for Discussion

○ Who do you think got the calf? Why?
○ Why do you think most of the animals agreed with the lion?
○ Who did the ape think should get the calf? How do you know?
○ If you had to decide, would you give the calf to the lion or the
  hyena? Why?
○ Do you know other stories about wise animals settling a problem
  for other animals? In this story which animal was wise?
○ In what ways was the lion a "bully"?
○ Were you ever in a situation in which you thought someone
  who had power over you was wrong? Did you agree with that
  person because you were afraid, or did you speak up?
○ Hold a trial to decide custody of the baby calf. Assign people to
  be the judge, lion, hyena, lion's lawyer, hyena's lawyer. Let the
  rest of the class be the jury.

WHY FEMALE MOSQUITOES BITE

Before you start to read

○ What is a mosquito? From the title, what do you know about mosquitoes?

○ Like the "The Ant and the Cicada," this story is written to explain something in nature. Looking at the title, what do you think this story will try to explain?

○ Read to the end of paragraph 5. What do you think will happen next?

○ Would you rather marry for love or money? When you read this story, see which choice the woman makes.

1.

2.

Why Female Mosquitoes Bite

Why Female Mosquitoes Bite

1   Many years ago in Vietnam, a poor fisherman lived with his wife. The fisherman was happy, but his beautiful wife was not. She wanted to be rich.

A

2   One day when the fisherman was working, his wife became sick and died. The fisherman came home and found his wife dead. He sat near her and prayed.

3   While he was praying, he heard a voice. The voice told him how to bring his wife back to life. The voice said, "Cut your finger and let three drops of blood fall on your wife." The man did what he was told. And when the third drop of blood fell on his wife, she came back to life. The fisherman was very happy to have his wife back.

4   One day soon after that, the wife went to the beach to wait for her husband to come back from fishing. While she was waiting, she met a rich man with a big boat. The rich man told the woman, "You are very beautiful. Come with me on my big boat. I can make you very wealthy." The woman wanted to be rich, so she went with him.

5   When her husband came back, he saw two other fishermen. They told him that his wife had left with the

rich man. The husband went to find his wife. When he found her, he was very angry. He asked her to come back home, but she would not. Then he told her that he wanted back his three drops of blood.

6   He cut her hand with a knife, and three drops of blood fell. Then the woman changed. She became very small and grew wings. She flew around her husband's head angrily saying, "Give me back the three drops of blood!"

7   To this day, female mosquitoes still fly around trying to get back those three drops of blood.

1.

2.

Exercises

True–False

1. _____ The wife was happy with her husband.
2. _____ The husband was a fisherman.
3. _____ The husband loved his wife.
4. _____ The fisherman was rich.
5. _____ The fisherman brought his wife back to life.
6. _____ The wife went with the rich man.
7. _____ The fisherman got his three drops of blood back.
8. _____ The wife turned into a mosquito.
9. _____ The wife was very beautiful.
10. _____ The man gave his wife four drops of blood.

Sentence Order

Put these sentences in the correct order.

1. _____ The wife went on the rich man's boat.
2. _____ The wife became sick and died.
3. _____ The wife became small and grew wings.
4. _____ The fisherman asked his wife to come back to him.
5. _____ The fisherman gave his wife three drops of blood.
6. _____ The fisherman went to find his wife.
7. _____ The fisherman cut his wife's hand.
8. _____ The fisherman prayed for his dead wife.

Comprehension

1. What was the husband's job?
2. Why wasn't the wife happy with her husband?
3. How did the husband learn how to bring his wife back to life?
4. How did the husband bring his wife back to life?
5. Where did the wife meet the rich man?
6. What happened to the wife when the husband took his blood back?
7. According to this story, why do female mosquitoes bite?
8. "The fisherman was happy, *but his beautiful wife was not*"(paragraph 1). What word is understood after *not*?
9. "The man did *what he was told*" (paragraph 3). What did he do?
10. "One day *soon after that*, the wife went to the beach" (paragraph 4). Soon after what?
11. "*But she would not*" (paragraph 5). Who is she? What wouldn't she do?
12. What word in paragraph 4 means the same as *rich*?

Related Words

Choose the correct form of the related words to put in the blanks.

die	**dies**	**died**
dead	**death**	**dying**

1. The woman became sick and _____.

2. Her husband came home and found her _____.

3. He was very upset about her _____, so he prayed for her.

4. Every day a child _____ from hunger somewhere in the world.

5. As he was _____, the thief told the police where he had hidden the money.

Vocabulary

Circle the words that describe the fisherman. Tell in which part of the story these words describe the fisherman. Use a dictionary for words you don't know.

happy	**praying**	**rich**	**poor**
angry	**greedy**	**vengeful**	**loving**

Circle the words that describe the wife. Tell where in the story they describe her.

unhappy	**beautiful**	**dead**	**greedy**	**rich**	**poor**
selfish	**vengeful**	**winged**			

Unusual Spellings and Plurals

<u>Kn</u> is pronounced <u>n</u> in <u>knife</u> List three other words in which <u>kn</u> is pronounced <u>n</u>.   1. _____   2. _____   3. _____

The plural of mosquit<u>o</u> is mosquit<u>oes</u>. Many words that end in *o* add *es* for the plural. List three other that words that end in <u>o</u> and add <u>es</u> to make the plural.   1. _____   2. _____   3. _____

Usually words add <u>s</u> to form plurals, but some plurals are irregular. For example, fisherman–fishermen. Write the plurals for the following words. You may want to use a dictionary.

Singular	Plural
wife	_____
knife	_____
life	_____

WHY FEMALE MOSQUITOES BITE

1   Many years ago in Vietnam, there lived a poor fisherman and his wife. The fisherman was happy, but his beautiful wife was not. She wanted to be wealthy.

2   One day while the husband was out fishing, the wife became ill and died. When he came home and found her dead, the fisherman was very sad. He sat near her and prayed.

3   While he was praying, he heard a voice telling him how to bring her back to life. The voice told him to cut his finger and let three drops of blood fall on his wife. The fisherman followed these instructions. As the third drop of blood fell on his wife, she came back to life. How happy he was to have his wife back!

4   One day shortly after that, the wife went down to the beach to wait for her husband to return from fishing. While she was waiting, she met a rich merchant with a large boat. The man told her that she was very beautiful and asked her to come with him on his big boat. He promised to make her rich, so she went with him.

5   When her husband returned, the other fishermen told him that his wife had gone off with the rich man. The

husband went to find his wife, and when he did, he was very angry. He asked her to come home, but she refused. Then he demanded that she give him back his three drops of blood. With a knife, he cut her hand.

6   When the third drop of blood fell, the woman changed. She became very tiny. She flew around her husband's head buzzing angrily and demanding that he give her back the three drops of blood.

7   And to this day, female mosquitoes still fly around trying to get back their blood!

Exercises

Antonyms

Circle the word in each group that means the *opposite* of the italicized word.

1. *husband*   spouse   mate   wife   brother

2. *poor*   penniless   rich   happy   money

3. *happy*   glad   smile   sad   tired

4. *tiny*   unusual   small   little   big

5. *dead*   tired   sick   alive   asleep

6. *refused*   answered   asked   agreed   denied

7. *ill*   sick   angry   dead   healthy

8. *beautiful*   ugly   sick   young   lovely

9. *return*   circle   leave   come back   turn around

10. *left*   went off   arrived   saw   loved

11. *female*   woman   male   wife   husband

Comprehension

1. "But his beautiful wife was not" (paragraph 1). What was she not?
2. The fisherman followed these instructions" (paragraph 3). What instructions did he follow?
3. Why did the wife go with the merchant?
4. "But she refused" (paragraph 5). What did she refuse to do?
5. Why do you think she refused?

6. What did her husband do when he found her dead? How did he know what to do?
7. What did her husband do when she refused to return with him?
8. According to this story, why do female mosquitoes bite?
9. "When he did, he was very angry" (paragraph 5). When he did what?
10. How did the wife change after her husband took back his three drops of blood?

Matching

Match the word in the first column with its definition in the second column.

1. _____ merchant
2. _____ refused
3. _____ demanded
4. _____ drop
5. _____ followed instructions
6. _____ mosquito
7. _____ wealthy
8. _____ buzzed
9. _____ ill
10. _____ tiny
11. _____ shortly
12. _____ bite
13. _____ beach

a. a small amount of liquid
b. a person who buys and sells goods
c. a little insect that bites
d. break the skin with teeth or stinger

e. soon
f. very small
g. rich
h. did as one was told
i. happy
j. said no
k. sick
l. asked for strongly
m. made a low noisy hum (like a bee)
n. shore

Vocabulary

Choose from the following words to fill in the blanks.

beach	buzzes	demanded	followed	gone off
ill	knife	merchant	mosquito	promised
pray	refused	returned	shortly	tiny
waiting	wealthy	wings	instructions	

1. Because the _____ was very

   _____, he owned a big boat.

2. Although the _____ is a very

   _____ insect, it annoys people when it

   _____ around their head.

3. When the poor people _____ food, the

   mean king _____ to get some for them.

4. When the fisherman learned that his wife had _____

   with a rich man, he _____ her.

Dictionary Definitions

Define each underlined word as it is used in the sentence.

1. The wife refused to come home.

   definition _____

   part of speech _____

   pronunciation _____

2. Please don't leave your refuse in front of my house.

   definition _____

   part of speech _____

   pronunciation _____

3. The saleswoman said, "I'll be with you <u>shortly</u>."

   definition _____

   part of speech _____

4. The customer replied <u>shortly</u>, "I want service now!"

   definition _____

   part of speech _____

5. There was a <u>buzz</u> in the room when the famous actress entered.

   definition _____

   part of speech _____

6. The child was scared by the bee <u>buzzing</u> around his head.

   definition _____

   part of speech _____

7. The boss <u>buzzed</u> his secretary to have her come to his office.

   definition _____

   part of speech _____

8. The wife had <u>gone off</u> with the merchant.

   definition _____

   part of speech _____

9. The fire alarm had <u>gone off</u> in the middle of the night.

   definition _____

   part of speech _____

10. The heat must have <u>gone off</u>; it's cold in here.

    definition _____

    part of speech _____

Exclamations

Sentences that are in exclamation form sometimes follow a different word order. *How* is followed by an adjective, and *what* is followed by a noun phrase. Then the noun and the verb phrase come at the end.

> **Normal word order:** He was happy to have his wife back.
>
> **Exclamation:** How happy he was to have his wife back!
>
> **Normal word order:** This is a great surprise.
>
> **Exclamation:** What a great surprise this is!

Change the following exclamations to regular sentences.

1. How good it is to see you!

   _____

2. What a good boy you are!

   _____

Change these sentences to exclamations.

3. That is a terrific idea.

   _____

4. You must be so happy about the new baby.

   _____

Topics for Discussion/Writing

- ○ Think of five adjectives to describe the wife. Talk about the wife's character. Do you think she is a good person? Why or why not?
- ○ Think of five adjectives to describe the husband. Talk about the husband's character. Do you think he was a good person? Why or why not?

- Was the husband right to take back the three drops of blood? Why or why not?
- What would you have done in the wife's place? What would you have done in the husband's place?
- How are the "The Ant and the Cicada," "The Mountain God and the River God," and "Why Female Mosquitoes Bite" alike? What natural event is explained by each story?
- What events in the story make it clear that the fisherman loved his wife?

THE SMARTEST ANIMAL

Before you start to read

○ What animal do you think is the smartest? Why?

○ Which do you think is better, brains (intelligence) or brawn(strength)? Why?

○ Read to the end of paragraph 4. How do you think the man will prove his intelligence? What do you think will happen next?

261

1.

2.

The Smartest Animal

THE SMARTEST ANIMAL

1   Once there was a farmer in Laos. Every morning and every evening he plowed his field with his buffalo.

2   One day a tiger saw the farmer and his buffalo working. The tiger was surprised to see a big animal listening to a small animal. He wanted to know more about the buffalo and the man.

3   After the man went home, the tiger spoke to the buffalo. "You are so big and strong. Why do you do everything that the man tells you?" The buffalo answered, "Oh, the man is very intelligent." The tiger asked, "Can you tell me how intelligent he is?" "No, I can't tell you," said the buffalo, "but you can ask him."

4   So the next day the tiger said to the man, "Can I see your intelligence?" But the man answered, "It's at home." "Can you go and get it?" asked the tiger. "Yes," said the man, "but I'm afraid you will kill my buffalo when I am gone. Can I tie you to a tree?"

5   After the man tied the tiger to the tree, he didn't go home to get his intelligence. He took his plow and hit the tiger. Then he said, "Now you *know* about my intelligence even if you haven't *seen* it."

263

Exercises

Dictionary Skills

Use your dictionary to define the underlined words as they are used in the sentences.

1. The man <u>plowed</u> his field every morning.

   definition _____

   part of speech _____

2. The man hit the tiger with his <u>plow</u>.

   definition _____

   part of speech _____

3. The businessman wore a jacket and <u>tie</u> to work.

   definition _____

   part of speech _____

4. Mrs. Claus <u>tied</u> all of the packages with red ribbon.

   definition _____

   part of speech _____

5. The baseball game was <u>tied</u> in the ninth inning.

   definition _____

   part of speech _____

6. The farmer planted crops in his <u>field</u>.

   definition _____

   part of speech _____

7. The football <u>field</u> was wet after the rain.

definition _____

part of speech _____

8. The baseball player <u>fielded</u> the ball.

definition _____

part of speech _____

Sentence Order

Put the following sentences in the correct order.

1. _____ The man hit the tiger with the plow.
2. _____ The buffalo said that the man was very intelligent.
3. _____ The man said that he had left his intelligence at home.
4. _____ The tiger saw the man plow his field with the buffalo.
5. _____ The tiger asked the buffalo a question.

Word Forms

Use the correct form of *intelligent* in each of the following sentences. You may use the same form more than once. Choose from:

intelligent **intelligently** **intelligence**

1. The man in the story was very _____.

2. He acted very _____ when he tied up the tiger.

3. The buffalo knew about the man's _____.

4. It was not very _____ of the tiger to let the man tie him up.

True–False

1. _____ The man really left his intelligence at home.
2. _____ The man went home to get his intelligence.
3. _____ The tiger wanted to eat the buffalo.
4. _____ The man tied up the tiger.
5. _____ The farmer plowed his field every morning and every evening.
6. _____ The farmer was intelligent.
7. _____ The buffalo was stronger than the man.

Synonyms and Antonyms

Circle the word in each group that is different from the others. You may use your dictionary.

1. intelligent   dumb   smart   wise
2. afraid   scared   brave   frightened
3. answered   replied   said   asked
4. listen to   obey   heed   disobey

Comprehension

1. The tiger was surprised to see a big animal listening to a small animal. What was the big animal? What was the small animal?
2. Why did the buffalo listen to the man?
3. What work did the buffalo do on the farm?
4. Where did this story take place?
5. Why did the man tie up the tiger?
6. Why did the man hit the tiger?
7. How did the tiger find out about the man's intelligence?
8. According to this story, what is the smartest animal?

THE SMARTEST ANIMAL

B

1   There was once a Laotian farmer who plowed his field every morning and every evening with his buffalo.

2   One day a tiger saw the farmer and the buffalo working together. The tiger was surprised to see such a big animal obeying such a small one. He was curious about the buffalo and the man.

3   After the man went home, the tiger went up to the buffalo and said, "I want to ask you something. You are so big and strong. Why do you obey the little man?" The buffalo answered, "Because the man is so intelligent." Then the tiger asked, "Can you tell me how intelligent he is?" "No, I can't tell you," said the buffalo, "but why don't you ask him?"

4   The next day the tiger asked the man to show him his intelligence. But the man answered that it was at home. The tiger asked the man to go home and get it. The man said that he would, but he would have to tie up the tiger so he couldn't hurt the buffalo. The tiger agreed.

5   But after he tied up the tiger, the man didn't go home to get his intelligence. Instead he took the plow and hit the tiger with it. Then he said, "Now you *know* about my intelligence, even if you haven't *seen* it."

Exercises

Vocabulary

Choose from the following words to fill in the blanks.

buffalo	**crop**	**curious**	**intelligence**
obey	**plow**	**tiger**	

1. The _____, like the ox and the horse, is an animal that farmers use to do work on a farm.

2. Before farmers can plant seeds, they must _____ the field.

3. Children do not always _____ their parents.

4. Sometimes being too _____ can get you in trouble.

5. _____ is another word for smartness.

Titles

A good title for this story would be:
- ○ The Buffalo and the Tiger
- ○ How the Man Proved His Intelligence
- ○ How the Buffalo Helps the Farmer

References

Tell what the underlined words refer to.

1. "The tiger was surprised to see such a <u>big animal</u> obeying such a <u>small one</u>." (paragraph 2)

   big animal _____   small one _____

2. "But why don't <u>you</u> ask <u>him</u>?"

   you _____   him _____

3. "The tiger asked the man to go home and get <u>it</u>." (paragraph 4)

   it _____

4. "The man said <u>he would</u>." (paragraph 4) Who is he?
   What would he do?

   he would _____

5. "The tiger <u>agreed</u>." (paragraph 4) What did he agree to?

   agreed _____

Descriptive Words

Put the following words under the animal they describe. Some words might describe more than one animal.

intelligent	strong	hardworking	big	smart
obedient	curious	small	sly	foolish

Tiger	Man	Buffalo
_____	_____	_____
_____	_____	_____
_____	_____	_____

Sentence Combining

1. The man went home. The tiger went up to the buffalo.

   (after) _____

2. A tiger saw a farmer and a buffalo. They were working together.

   (leave out words) _____

3. The tiger was surprised. He saw such a big animal obeying such a small one.

   (use the infinitive) _____

4. He saw a big animal. It was obeying a small one.

   (omit words) _____

5. There was once a Laotian farmer. He plowed his field every day.

   (who) _____

Review of Reported Speech and Direct Speech

Change the following sentences to direct speech. The first one is done for you.

1. The tiger asked the man to show him his intelligence.

   The tiger asked the man, "Will you show me your intelligence?"

2. But the man answered that it was at home.

   _____

3. The tiger asked the man to go home and get it.

   _____

4. The man said that he would but he would have to tie up the tiger so he couldn't hurt the buffalo.

   _____

5. The tiger agreed.

   _____

Change the following sentences to reported speech.

1. The tiger said to the buffalo, "I want to ask you something."
   <u>The tiger said that he wanted to ask the buffalo something.</u>

2. The tiger asked the buffalo, "Why do you obey the little man?"

   _____

3. The buffalo answered, "Because the man is so intelligent."

   _____

Idioms

The expression *tie up* has several meanings. Define that phrase the way it is used in the following sentences.

1. I'd like to meet with you, but I'm <u>tied up</u> today.
   definition _____

2. The thief <u>tied up</u> the man after stealing his money.
   definition _____

3. The baseball team <u>tied up</u> the game in the bottom of the ninth inning.
   definition _____

Topics for Discussion

○ Animals have appeared in many of the stories in this book. Some of them are: ant, cicada, hare, tortoise, ape; lion; hyena; buffalo; billy goat; fox; stork; parrot; tiger.

Which of those animals were hardworking?

Which were persistent?

Which were strong?

Which were smart?

Which were lazy?

Which were greedy or mean?

Which were little?

Which were big?

Which could fly?

Which could run fast?

○ According to this story, what is the smartest animal? Do you agree? Why?

○ In this story, which animal had brains (intelligence)? Which animal had brawn (strength)? Which do you think is more important for success? Why?

○ Retell this story from the point of view of the tiger.

○ Retell this story from the man's point of view.

GLOSSARY

accident (n) something bad that happens and is not planned

accuse (v) to say someone did wrong, to blame

alike (adj) similar, the same; (adv) in the same way

amazed (adj) surprised

angry (adj) annoyed, irritated

ant (n), a small insect that lives on the ground and is famous for hard work

anthill (n) a small hill(raised pile of earth) that ants build to live in

ape (n) large monkey

appear (v) to become able to be seen; to become visible

areca tree (n) a tall palm tree with white flowers from Southeast Asia

argument (n) disagreement

arrest (v) to stop someone; to stop someone who is breaking the law, to put someone in jail

ask for the hand of (v) to ask to marry

astonished (adj) surprised

attack (v) to act against, usually with violence

awake (v), to stop sleeping; to wake up

awoke past tense of awake

ax (n), tool used to cut down trees

bag (n) something to hold or carry things, made of cloth, leather, or paper, and open at the top

banquet (n) formal dinner for many people

bargain (n) agreement to do or give something in return for something else

beach (n), a sandy shore of an ocean, sea, lake, or river

beast (n), animal

beg (v, to ask for something

belong to (v) be owned by

betel vine (n), climbing plant from Asia

billy goat (n),male goat

blanket (n) warm cover used on beds

borrow (v) to take something for a certain length of time

bow and arrow (n) a kind of weapon
   bow: a piece of wood held in a curve and used for shooting arrows
   arrow: thin straight stick, pointed at one end, that is shot from a bow

273

bowl (n) deep, round dish for holding food or liquids

bring (v) to take or carry

brought past tense of **bring**

buffalo (n) large, cowlike animal

bull (n) a male cow

buzzing (v) a noise made by bees, mosquitoes, and other insects

chat (v) to talk in a friendly, informal manner

check (v) to see if something is okay; to make sure

chilly (adj) cool, cold enough to be uncomfortable

cicada (n) a kind of insect

claim (v) to say something is true

complete (adj), finished

confused (adj), mixed up; not sure

contest (n) a fight or competition

convinced (v) to be persuaded; to believe

corn (n) (in American English) tall plant whose yellow grains are used for food, called *maize* in British English

countryside (n) land outside cities and towns

court (n room or building where law cases can be heard and judged (decided)

cramp (n) a sharp or strong pain that makes movement difficult

crawl (v) to move slowly on hands and knees, or with body close to the ground

crime (n) an act that is against the law

crop (n) a plant such as grain, fruits or vegetables grown by a farmer

custom (n) a tradition

damp (adj) a little wet

daughter (n) a female child

dead (adj) no longer alive

delicious (adj) tasting very good, tasty

demand (v) to ask for (something) strongly

dig (v) to break up and move earth; to make a hole by taking away earth

disagree (v) to have different opinions

disappear (v) to go out of sight, become invisible

distance (n) separation in space, the space separating two things

drown (v) to die under water from lack of air

eagerly (adv), with great interest

empty (adj) with nothing inside, the opposite of *full*

enter (v) to come or go into

exchange (v) to give something in return for something else

expect (v) to think, believe, hope(something will happen)

farmer (n) person who grows crops or raises animals

fault (n) mistake, responsibility for a mistake

fellow (n) a man

field (n) piece of land used for animals or crops

file (n) steel tool with a rough side used for smoothing or cutting other surfaces

finish line (n) the place where a race ends

fisherman (n), someone who catches fish

flow (v) to run or spread (as liquid)

fool (n) silly person

forgive (v), to stop being angry about something; to excuse someone

fox (n) small wild animal, similar to a wolf in size

generous (adj) ready to give money or help

gentle (adj) kind, soft

get even (v) to get back at, to make things even

goat (n) four-legged animal, usually domesticated

gourd (n) large fruit with a hard shell that grows on a vine

grandchild (n), the child of a person's son or daughter

granted (adj) given

grateful (adj) feeling or showing thanks to someone

greedy (adj) wanting more than what is fair

greet (v) to say hello, to welcome when meeting

ground (n) earth, soil

hare (n) animal like a rabbit, able to run fast

harvest (v) to pick crops

highlands (n) an area of mountains

honest (adj) truthful

horns (n), two hard, pointed growths on the top of the heads of goats, sheep, cattle, and many wild animals

hurt (v) to cause or give pain

hyena (n) doglike animal of Africa and Asia that makes a sound like a laugh

identical (adj) exactly the same

identify (v) to show who or what a particular person or thing is

industrious (adj) hardworking

insect (n) small animal with no bones and a hard outer cover, having six legs and a body with three parts

instructions (n) explanation or directions that tell how to do something

intelligent (adj) very smart

invite (v) to ask someone to go somewhere or do something

iron (n) common and useful metal, used in making steel

jail (n) place where criminals are kept, prison

jealous (adj) wanting to get what someone else has

judge (v) to decide; (n) person who decides in court

lay down (v), past tense of **lie down**

lazy (adj) describing someone who does not like activity or work

lend (v) give something for a certain amount of time

lie down (v) to put one's body in a flat position

limestone (n) type of stone used in making cement

lion (n) a large wild animal of the cat family

Midas touch (n) ability to turn things into gold, the ability to succeed or to become rich in business

miss (v) to feel unhappy because someone is not near

mistake (n) error, something done incorrectly

mixed up (adj) confused

mosquito (n) small flying insect that drinks blood

native town (n) the place where one is born

needle (n) long, pointed metal pin with a hole in one end for the thread used in sewing

neighbor (n) person who lives near another person

notice (v) to see something, to be aware of something

nowadays (adv) at the present time

obey (v) to do what one is told to do

orphaned (adj) having no mother or father

oversleep (v) to sleep too long or too late

overtake (v) to pass someone or something

pain (n) feeling of hurt in a particular part of the body

pair (n) two things that go together

parrot (n) tropical bird that can copy human speech

patient (adj) having the ability to wait calmly without complaining

pitcher (n) container for holding liquids with a handle and a lip(spout) for pouring

plain (adj) not good-looking; not fancy

plow (n) farming tool used to break up and turn over the earth

possess (v) to have, to own

powder (n), something in the form of very small, dry grains

powerful (adj) strong

pray (v) to ask God for something, to talk to the gods

pregnant (adj) expecting a baby

prepare (v) to get ready

princess (n) the daughter of a king

prison (n) a jail or place where criminals are kept

promptly (adv) on time, quickly

promise (v) to say something that another person can believe or depend on

pumpkin (n) plant with a large orange-colored fruit that grows on the ground

rabbit (n) a small animal with large ears that hops quickly

race (n, a competition in speed to see who is the fastest

reach (v) to arrive at, to get to

realize (v) to understand and believe (a fact)

refuse (v) not to accept or do or give; to say "no"

repeat (v) to say again

request (n) polite demand; (v), to ask for nicely

rescue (v) to save from danger; set free

response (n) answer

rich (adj) having a lot of money; wealthy

ripe (adj) mature, fully grown

rise (v) to go up, to get higher

rivalry (n) competition

roll (v) to move by turning over and over

satisfied (adj) pleased, happy, having enough

scoop (n) deep, round spoon

scream (v) to cry angrily and loudly

several (determiner) a few but not many; some

señor (n) a Spanish word that means "Mr." or "man"

shadow (n) dark area where direct light is blocked

sharp (adj) having a thin cutting edge or fine point

sharpen (v) to make sharp or able to cut

shine (v) to give off light, to look bright

shiver (v) to shake from cold or fear

shocked (adj) very surprised

shortly (adv) soon

smashed (adj) broken into pieces (by force); (v) broke into pieces

starting line (n) the place where a race begins

starving (adj) very hungry, dying from hunger

steadily (adv) with firm, sure movements

steal (v) to take something that belongs to another person

stitch (v) to sew with a needle and thread

stork (n) large bird with a long beak, neck, and legs

stranger (n) person who is unfamiliar, not known

succeed (v) to do well

suggest (v) to say or write an idea

sure enough (adv) certainly

swallow (n) small bird with pointed wings

swim (v) the act of moving through water by moving one's arms and legs

thief (n) a person who takes things that belong to other people

thread (n) very thin string or cord used in sewing

tiger (n) large striped wild animal of the cat family

tiny (adj) very small

tomato (n) soft red fruit eaten as a vegetable

tortoise (n) slow-moving land animal with a soft body covered by a hard shell(similar to a turtle)

unfaithful (adj) not loyal to one's husband or wife

unique (adj) unusual, one of a kind

unpopular (adj) not well-liked, not liked by many people

upset (adj) worried, unhappy about something

village (n) group of houses in a country area, smaller than a town

water buffalo (n) large animal with horns that is often used to work on farms

wealthy (adj) rich

wing (n) the part of an insect or bird that helps it fly

wise (adj) having a good sense of judgment, able to understand what happens and decide the right action

wolf (n) wild animal of the dog family that hunts other animals

world (n), the earth and its inhabitants

worried (adj) thinking about a problem, concerned, anxious